# BIG CYPRESS

*A Changing Seminole Community*

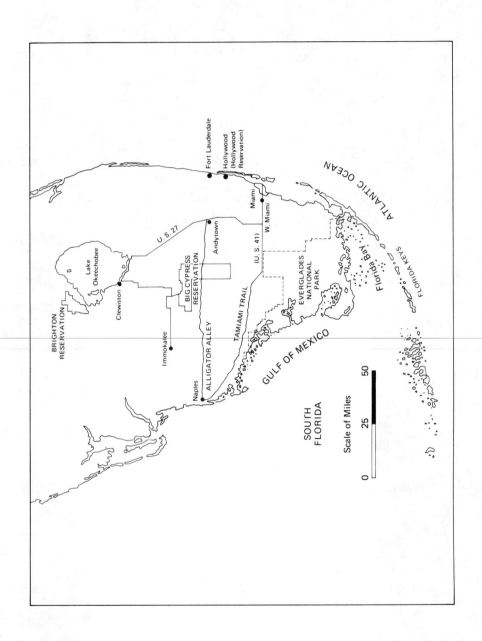

SOUTH FLORIDA

Scale of Miles

0    25    50

# BIG CYPRESS

## *A Changing Seminole*

## *Community*

By

**MERWYN S. GARBARINO**
*University of Illinois at Chicago*

**WAVELAND**

**PRESS, INC.**

Prospect Heights, Illinois

For information about this book, write or call:

Waveland Press, Inc.
P.O. Box 400
Prospect Heights, Illinois 60070
(708) 634-0081

*To my mother and father*

**Cover photo:** Seminole Indian women in traditional dress standing before platform house (chickee).

ISBN 0-88133-211-9

Printed in the United States of America

7  6  5  4  3  2

# Foreword

## About the Author

Merwyn Stephens Garbarino received her Ph.D. in anthropology from Northwestern University and is professor of anthropology at the University of Illinois at Chicago where she has been teaching since 1966. After fieldwork among the Mikasuki-speaking Seminole Indians of south Florida, Dr. Garbarino did fieldwork on reservations in the northern plains and the upper Great Lakes. More recently she has done research on Indian urbanization in Chicago. Her theoretical interests include epistemology, the history of ethnology, and the interpretation of anthropological data and concepts for those who are not majors in anthropology. Dr. Garbarino is author of *Sociocultural Theory in Anthropology: A Short History* and *Native American Heritage, Second Edition,* and co-author of *People and Cultures,* a textbook for junior high school social science courses.

## About the Book

The Seminole have long been of interest to the general public, as well as to anthropologists, and yet there has been very little reliable literature easily available to anyone but serious scholars. *Big Cypress* makes available to students and others a general treatment of life in one Seminole community with a special focus upon culture change and decision-making. Until the late 1950s this group had been isolated from tourists due to lack of paved roads and completely cut off from contact with the outside world during the rainy season. Professor Garbarino was able to observe changes resulting from increasing contact with the outside world after a major surfaced road was opened. This case study includes, therefore, both ethnographic description of Big Cypress and an analysis of significant dimensions of change.

The author focuses on important changes that took place, such as the introduction of the cattle industry and the development of a new political structure. This study should be particularly useful to those interested in the practical application of anthropological studies, since it contains detailed materials concerning what actually happened to the individual Seminoles in the process of becoming cattlemen, the misconceptions arising from the Indians' lack of technological and financial training, and the lack of communication between the residents of the reservation and the agency personnel.

Professor Garbarino includes an analysis of the decision-making process, as it is of prime importance in this situation. The strong tradition of autonomy existing in each Seminole group and the individualistic orientation make it virtually impossible for the communities to make decisions without outside pressure. Complete unanimity must be obtained by the decision-making body before a decision can be made. The Seminole believe that majority rule makes for a discontented minority.

The book also deals with the problem of the alienation of the young. Parallels can be drawn for our own culture from this situation, where cultural deterrents and rewards are insufficient to curtail individual aggression.

George and Louise Spindler

# Acknowledgments

I wish to express my deep appreciation to the National Science Foundation for financial support during my fieldwork period in 1964–1965, and to the Social Science Research Council for support in 1967. Without those grants I could not have undertaken the work.

My gratitude goes to all the Big Cypress residents who so graciously allowed me to live with them and who made that sojourn informative and pleasant. I hope they will be pleased with what I have written.

My intellectual debts are too extensive to acknowledge individually. However, I wish to thank Dr. Ronald Cohen of Northwestern University, Dr. James Van Stone of the Field Museum of Natural History, and Dr. William Shack of the University of California, Berkeley, for reading early versions of this manuscript and making many valuable suggestions. I also want to thank Mr. Richard Moret whose editorial advice was of the greatest aid in getting the manuscript ready for publication. Finally, I owe a great deal to the typists, Mrs. Francine Harrell and Miss Rita Miller.

MERWYN S. GARBARINO

# Contents

# 1

# Introduction

**B**IG CYPRESS is one of four federal reservations for the Florida Seminole. The other three are Brighton Reservation, Hollywood Reservation, and the Miccosukee[1] Reservation which consists of scattered plots along U. S. Highway 41, called the Tamiami Trail by the Indians. Residents of all four reservations are collectively referred to as Seminole Indians, but there are two distinct linguistic groups: Mikasuki, spoken at Big Cypress, Hollywood, and along the Trail; and Muskogee, spoken at Brighton.

Not only are the Seminole a post-Columbian group, but the use of the name "Seminole" appears not to have been widely used until 1750. When Ponce de Leon arrived in Florida in 1513, the important groups of Indian people were the Calusa in the south, the Ais on the southeast coast, the Timucua in the central north, and the Apalachee in the northwest. By the eighteenth century, pestilence and war had left only wandering remnants of these aboriginal Florida tribes.

Into the vacuum moved several Indian groups fleeing white soldiers and settlers in the area just north of the peninsula or seeking relief from attacks by other Indian groups who were suffering under pressures from other white invaders. When the Yamassee were driven out of Carolinas in 1715, they drifted south into the Florida area, and the Hitchiti-speaking Oconee moved down the Apalachicola River to settle there. These two, with an uncertain number of other peoples, came to be know as "Seminole," which means "wild" or "undomesticated," but not "renegated" or "runaway" as is sometimes stated. The Hitichiti speakers came to be called the Mikasuki, the term derived from the dialect they spoke.

Creek speakers of a related language, Muskogee, from the town of Eufala, moved north of Tampa Bay in 1767, and the Creek War of 1813–1814, caused an influx of other Creek who joined the loose confederation of "Seminole" groups

---

[1] There are at least four spellings of this word: Mikasuki, Mickasukie, Miccosukee, Mekusukey. Except for proper names which have been standardized in print, as in the case of the Miccosukee Tribe, I shall use the anthropological spelling, Mikasuki, which is standard in the literature and is used by linguists also.

1

*North Entrance to the reservation.*

and tripled their number. Hitchiti and Muskogee are both languages of the Musk-hogean stock, but they are mutually unintelligible. However, the situation was such that the people were united in their response to their common foe, the young United States.

I first saw Big Cypress Reservation in 1963, and since that initial visit, I have been back seven times. This book contains what I have learned of the inhabitants of Big Cypress. It is not intended as a complete history or ethnography of the Seminole Indians of Florida, but rather it is the story of one community of Seminole as they are living and changing in the mid-twentieth century.

The Seminole Indians at Big Cypress are interesting for a number of reasons. First, very little has been written about this community because so little has been known about it until fairly recently. Because there was no paved road until the late 1950s, Big Cypress was virtually cut off from the rest of the area during the rainy season and remained isolated from the tourist sections of Florida. I arrived at Big Cypress shortly after the road from Clewiston had been paved, but the road to Immokalee was still sand and marl. Having been mired down on the Immokalee road during my first season living at Big Cypress, I can vouch for the difficulties of travel in the days before paved roads.

Another reason which makes Big Cypress so appealing for anyone inter-ested in American Indians is the preservation of many traditional ways which are being lost or greatly changed by Indians in more frequent contact with the dominant society. The Big Cypress people have maintained their language. None of the Seminole Indians in Oklahoma speak Mikasuki now. The language the Oklahoma Indians speak is Muskogee, as mentioned, a related but mutually unintelligible tongue. Along with the language, the Big Cypress people have preserved a number of customs which I will describe in this book.

A third reason for finding the Big Cypress people so interesting is the change resulting from increasing contact with outside society. At the time I first saw Big Cypress there were plans to build a toll road across the southern part of the reservation, and an access road was planned to connect the toll road with the village on the reservation. Political conflict between state and county resulted in so much delay that although the toll road, which has been named Alligator Alley, was finished by the time I was doing research in Florida in 1968, the access road was still under construction and the target date for its completion was nearly a year off. (It was completed early in 1970.) Nevertheless, the Big Cypress residents were able to drive along the banks of one of the canals which cross the area bringing water from Lake Okeechobee to Miami, and from the banks of the canal drive up onto the toll road. This substitute for an access road was feasible only in dry weather. With the completion of the access road, contact with the coast should speed up changes on the reservation even more.

William Sturtevant studied the medical practices of the Big Cypress Seminole for his doctoral dissertation (Sturtevant 1954); but he did not include a general treatment of the society and culture. He says:

> Although an occasional man may be found who is willing to converse quite extensively with an outsider, I have met no woman over thirty years old, and very few under, who will talk at all to an outsider. . . .
> . . . it seems impossible to live in a Mikasuki camp . . . (Sturtevant 1954:12).

That statement alone shows by contrast to my experience that a very great change had already taken place in the decade between his visit and mine.

Although the Mikasuki have the reputation of being unfriendly, I found no trace of this. Nor did I find any of the reticence described by Sturtevant. The people seemed very shy at first, but they were always gracious and pleasant, and almost everyone seemed interested in what I was doing on the reservation. In the years that followed I believe that people saw me so often that they took my presence for granted, and I now count a number of people living at Big Cypress as my friends.

A promising topic for study was economic change resulting from the development of the cattle industry. Individual Indians had bought cattle as early as 1953, but it was not until the government established a revolving credit plan and cattle loans for individuals that any large herds were pastured at Big Cypress. After the development of a working credit program, an Indian could apply for a loan which would then be applied to the purchase of a herd of breeding cows, and which, through the process of calf production and sales, was expected to be self-liquidating. The simplicity was appealing, and cattle programs had been started on western reservations successfully. However, the problems of land development were very different in the south Florida swampland, and those problems became the object of my study during two of the periods I spent at Big Cypress.

With the changing economic situation came a new political structure. The Indians voted in 1957 to incorporate under the Wheeler-Howard Act of 1934, known as the Indian Reorganization Act. Until 1957 there had been no organized political structure among the Seminole to provide leadership to oversee the use of reservation lands and money held in trust. The Indians themselves had had very little voice in planning. The incorporation in 1957 enabled the Indians to have representatives to make decisions on expenditures and improvements and to have a voice in the general direction of the cattle industry.

I lived on the reservation for about 18 months altogether, and I talked to every adult there. I lived with different families, one of which had no English speaking members. Early in my stay I made a map of the camp sites on the reservation and took a census by visiting each camp and getting the information from one of the adult members. The census data included not only the population size, but also such facts as who were English speakers, who owned cattle, what crops were cultivated, which electrical appliances were being used, and who had cars. I also acquired information on clan membership, employment, income, and levels of education. In the process of visiting all the camps, I made my presence known to the people of Big Cypress. The second season in the field I administered a questionnaire to all the inhabitants who owned cattle or who had owned cattle. No sampling procedures were used since the population, between 260 and 300, was small enough to interview everyone. I used an interpreter for all but six of the scheduled interviews because not many adults knew more than a few words of English, although they understood far more than they could speak. My competence in Mikasuki was of the same degree. I learned to understand a conversation, but my speech usually brought laughter or tolerant smiles. For visiting and general observation I did not have interpreters, but for the accuracy of the questionnaires I found an interpreter essential.

Although I spent my first two visits at Big Cypress studying primarily the cattle economy and political structure, I also learned about daily life and problems. Living in a household it is impossible not to be absorbed into the life-ways of the people. I became especially interested in the problems of the educated person who decides to return to the reservation. I did a study on one woman who had left to go to business college and work, and who then returned to live again at Big Cypress (Garbarino 1970).

In addition to being a participant observer on the reservation, I spent two weeks at the Seminole agency at Hollywood, Florida, to research the official records. That research involved reading credit accounts of the Big Cypress people to determine economic characteristics; examining the minutes, resolutions, and ordinances of the tribal council and board of directors; and reading the minutes of the Cattlemen's Association. I also made a survey of the voting records which were, unfortunately, incomplete. Nevertheless, the written documents gave me information about the incomes, employment, welfare, credit ratings, decision-making, and voting which I could not obtain through discussion with the people, most of whom kept no records because they were illiterate.

My first objecive was to isolate and describe the decision-making structure operating during the change to a cattle economy. I was looking for answers to two questions: How does a society make a major economic change? What happens to traditional patterns in political relationships when such a change occurs? In addition I wanted to learn what communication lines existed among members of the society and between the society and external groups.

The decisional method offered the opportunity to study power empirically through a time and process analysis rather than through a static situation or interpersonal relations study (Garbarino 1967). In addition, the decisional method produced information about the acculturative process since the decisions made concerning the cattle program almost always involved the introduction of new techniques, and changes in interpersonal relationships and material culture.

The recruitment of leaders in this changing tribal society was a peripheral finding. I have also compared and contrasted the decision-makers with the general Indian population. I confined the study to policy making in the cattle program to keep the field from becoming unwieldy and to keep it of workable size for investigation by a single person. After a few months in residence at Big Cypress I had definite opinions about the connection between authority and income, and about the general Indian attitude toward the cattle program. It was my opinion that leadership was determined largely, if not completely, by socioeconomic status and that the cattle owners all considered the cattle program to be immensely successful. As I began to focus my attention more specifically on the cattle program, I discovered that both opinions were at least partially erroneous.

The research plan involved studying one specific decision to describe and analyze its stages and participants. I was fortunately in the field during the period a major decision was made for the cattle program. This one decision required three years of negotiation, and I depended upon the memories of people participating as well as upon written data gathered from minutes of meetings. I also was in the field living in the household of one of the decision-makers, a particularly favorable position for close observation, so many of my conclusions were reached as a result of studying actual decision-making behavior as a participant-observer.

I found a new world at Big Cypress, and my life will never be quite the same again. I would like to think that readers of this book see Big Cypress as a success story because that is what it is. There have been many problems and many hardships, but the people have been solving their problems, and they have often solved them without the deadening dependence on the Bureau of Indian Affairs paternalism which has so often tended to stifle initiative and creativity on reservations. One cannot help but admire the independent spirit which the people have displayed on so many occasions, standing up for their right to make a choice in their own way. I hope that this independence comes through in the following pages. It is all too easy to stress the failures, the difficulties, the bewilderment since those aspects are what we so often look for in culture change. All too often the solid but unexciting increments of achievement are not recorded or are glossed over. Big Cypress society has achieved so much. The people are making their own life-style, taking what seems valuable to them both from the dominant society and from their own traditional ways. And, most important, they are making the selection for themselves. That they still have many problems to solve is true, but where is the society without problems.

When my friends at Big Cypress read this, I hope that they will be pleased with what I have written because it was written truthfully, but with affection and admiration. Big Cypress is a community with problems, but it is also a community with promise.

All the quotations in the body of this study are statements made to me by informants unless otherwise noted. The names of the people have been changed because the informants were promised anonymity.

# 2

# The Background

## History

REFERRING TO THE MANY TRIBES which formed the Seminole, Swanton says: "The different elements among the Seminole have fused so completely that in only a few cases can they be separated. The name is little more than a convenient term, a historical vestige applied after all substance has departed (Swanton 1922:179).

To get an overall picture of how this fusion came about, it is necessary to go back in time to the pre-Columbian days and review the aboriginal tribes of Florida. In the northern part of Florida, extending into what is now Georgia, were the Timucua. The present city of Ocala is a place name derived from the Timucuan town, Ocale. On the western coast of Florida from Timucuan territory down into the Keys there was a group of related tribelets or towns collectively known as the Calusa. The Calusa built seaworthy dugout canoes in which they traveled through the Keys and to Cuba. Bartram says they crossed to the Bahama Islands as well (Bartram 1958:143, and see Swanton's note in Bartram:373). There were independent tribal units on the east coast: the Tekesta near the present-day site of Miami, the Ais near what is now called Indian River Inlet, and the Jeaga between those two groups. The territory around the Florida capital, Tallahassee (itself an Indian word meaning "Big Town") was occupied by the Apalachee.

Ponce de Leon, who gave the name "Florida" to the peninsula, first sighted the land in 1513. In 1521 he died in Cuba as a result of wounds inflicted by Indians when he landed on the west coast of Florida, near Apalachee Bay. Francisco de Garay, another Spaniard to contact the Florida Indians in very early times, mapped the coast of the Gulf of Mexico from Florida to the Panuco River in 1519. Among the explorers penetrating the interior were Pánfilo de Navarez and Alvar Nunez Cabeza de Vaca who landed near Tampa Bay in 1528. In 1539 an expedition under Hernando de Soto also started from Tampa Bay and passed northward into Apalachee territory and from there westward toward the Mississippi River. These Spaniards were explorers, not settlers, and they made little attempt to wrest the land from the Indian tribes, although relations were not always peaceful. The Spaniards were interested in exploration and in establishing a series of forts at strategic spots along the coast to protect their sailing vessels on the way back to Spain. The coastal waters were often dangerous, and the Strait of Florida between Cuba and the mainland rapidly became a favorite place for privateers to lie in wait for the gold- and silver-laden Spanish ships returning to the Old World.

In 1562 there was an effort to press French claims in Florida, and for a short period French Huguenots attempted living at Fort Caroline, a site which they established on the St. John's River. It was during the French occupation that the artist Jacques Le Moyne made his sketches which add so much to our information about the Indian population of the time. In September of 1565 the settlement was captured by Spaniards, and the French never succeeded in establishing another settlement in Florida. Le Moyne escaped from the Spanish forces and made his way back to France. The French had established unusually good relations with the Indians and the records kept by Réné Goulâine de Laudonnier, who escaped with Le Moyne, as well as Le Moyne's pictures are the finest sources of ethnological information about the ancient Florida Indians, far more detailed and accurate than the Spanish accounts.

More successful belligerents against Spain were the British. Sir Francis Drake destroyed the Spanish city of St. Augustine in 1586. It was rebuilt by the Spanish and plundered again by an English buccanneer, John Davis, in 1665. The Indians in the northern area sometimes aided English aggressions against Spain, and finally with the British destruction of the missions and with the Spanish need to ransom Cuba from Britain, Spain abandonned Florida to the British who administered it in two parts, East and West Florida, from 1763 to 1783. Under British rule land grants were made to induce white settlements, which later swelled with British refugees after the American Revolutionary War. Florida was surrendered to Spain once again under pressure from the United States of America, but Spanish control over the area declined as her power in the New World declined. Andrew Jackson invaded Florida in 1818, and it became a part of the United States in 1821.

During Spanish occupancy, Spanish-Indian relations were at first hostile, but they slowly improved, and many Indians in the north were converted to Catholic Christianity by Spanish missionaries. However, the Spaniards brought disease as well as religion. Swanton (1922:338) quotes a letter dated January 17, 1617, stating that half of the Indians had died of pestilence in the preceding four years.

Death by epidemic increased in the seventeenth century and was augmented by fighting among Florida Indians and Indians from the north where the British were settling, as well as between Indians and Spanish. The English in the late seventeenth and early eighteenth centuries were marauding along the Carolina-

Florida border. They had been raiding for slaves throughout the southeast, and when they decided to take a census of the Indian population in the colony of South Carolina, the Indians suspected it was a prelude to an attempt at enslaving them. The result was an uprising in 1715 which has been called the Yamassee War, although a number of other southeastern tribes in addition to the Yamasee participated. The colonial soldiers made short work of this uprising and large numbers of Yamassee and other Indians moved down into Florida. The British raiding and general persecution caused the Yamassee to seek alliance with the Spanish.

> Under date of July, 1754, the Colonial Records of Georgia speak of the Yamassee as still allied with the Spaniards, and about the year 1761, we hear of a few Yamassee, about 20 men near St. Augustine.
> Meantime, however, they were being harrassed continually by the Creek Indians in alliance with the English, and presently some Creeks began to move into the peninsula and make permanent homes there (Swanton 1922:106).

Bartram (1958:118) refers to Yamassee living among the Seminole as slaves in 1774. However, as will be shown later, the Seminole and other southeastern Indians married their slaves, and their children were born free.

During the seventeenth and eighteenth centuries European-Indian contact was largely confined to the north, and south Florida Indians had little to do with Europeans except for shipwrecks and castaways and occasional meetings between small groups of Spanish soldiers and Ais Indians. It is reported that the chief of the Ais visited St. Augustine in 1609 (Swanton 1922:343), at which time he was baptized. The Indians in the south asked for missionaries and some plans were made by the Spanish to missionize, but the Calusa and other southern Indians remained unconverted at the time of the British takeover of Florida. During that year, 1763, many of the remaining Calusa went to Cuba to live (Swanton 1922:343).

To put it simply, as a result of contact with European diseases, the aboriginal population of northern Florida was greatly decreased. In fact, when the first people to be called Seminole finally moved into the peninsula and down toward the Everglades, the area was largely uninhabited. The term "Seminole," indicating a social or political unit, was in use by the mid-eighteenth century, and it was applied to various people who were descendants of a number of different southeastern tribes which had mingled with one another and with the remains of the earlier Florida groups.

> Although now reckoned as one of the "Five Civilized Tribes," the name Seminole is applied to a body of Indians of very modern origin. The nucleus consisted of the Oconee Indians, whose home (about 1695–1715) was on Oconee River, Ga., but who moved to the Lower Creek country about 1715, and 30 or 40 years later entered Florida and established themselves on the Alachua prairie. They were the Hitchiti, and except for a band of Eufaula, the first tribes to join them were of this same connection, including some Sawokli, Tamathli, Apalachicola, Hitchiti, and Chiaha, a part of whom soon came to be known as Mikasuki though under what circumstances is unknown (Swanton 1946:181).

Swanton gives more information about the Oconee in his commentary to Bartram:

> In the early part of the eighteenth century they lived upon the Oconee River and were known as the Oconee tribe. Their chief, Cowkeeper, was at that time constantly leading raiding parties against the Spaniards and Spanish Indians in Florida. Subsequently he and his people moved to the Creek towns on the Chattahoochee where part continued as late as 1799. Before that time however, the chief and another part of the tribe moved to the Alachua country where Bartram found them in the town of Cuscowilla. Cowkeeper and his tribe retained, partly from this priority, the primacy also in the Seminole Nation and all of the head chiefs of the Seminole until the removal were descended from Cowkeeper in the female line (Bartram 1958:336, 337 [commentary by Swanton]).

Bartram was a naturalist who traveled through Florida in 1774 while it was still British territory. His descriptions of the Seminole of that time are the major source of information on the group during the British occupancy, and they will be quoted at some length.

The following is a description of an early Seminole (which he spells "Siminole") village on the west shore of St. John's River:

> As I continued coasting the Indian shore of this bay, on doubling a promontory, I suddenly saw before me an Indian settlement, or village. It was a fine situation, the bank rising gradually from the water. There were eight or ten habitations, in a row, or street, fronting the water, and about fifty yards distance from it. Some of the youth were naked up to their hips in the water, fishing with rods and lines, whilst others, younger, were diverting themselves in shooting frogs with bows and arrows. On my near approach, the little children took to their heels, and ran to some women, who were hoeing corn; but the stouter youth stood their ground, under the cool shade of spreading Oaks and Palms, that were ranged in front of their houses; they arose, and eyed me as I passed, but perceiving that I kept on, without stopping, they resumed their former position. They were civil, and appeared happy in their situation.
>
> There was a large Orange grove at the upper end of their village; the trees were large, carefully pruned, and the ground under them clean, open, and airy. There seemed to be several hundred acres of cleared land, about the village; a considerable portion of which was planted, chiefly with corn (Zea), Batatas, Beans, Pompions, Squashes, (Curcurbita verrucosa) Melons (Cucurbita citrullus) Tobacco (Nicotiana) etc., abundantly sufficient for the inhabitants of the village (Bartram 1958:59, 60).

Bartram remarked upon the Spanish influence among the Seminole:

> The manners and customs of the Alachuas, the most of the lower Creeks or Siminoles, appear evidently tinctured with Spanish civilization. Their religious and civil usuages manifest a predilection for the Spanish customs. There are several Christians among them, many of whom wear little silver crucifixes, affixed to a wampum collar around their necks, or suspended by a small chain upon their breast. These are said to be baptized, and notwithstanding most of them speak and understand Spanish, yet they have been the most bitter and formidable Indian enemies the Spanish have ever had. The slaves, both male and females, are permitted to marry amongst them: their children are born free, and considered in

every respect equal to themselves, but the parents continue in a state of slavery as long as they live (Bartram 1958:118, 119).

The Siminoles, but a weak people, with respect to numbers, all of them I suppose would not be sufficient to people one of the towns in the Muscogulge (for instance, the Uches on the main branch of the Apalachucla river, which alone contains near two thousand inhabitants.) Yet this handful of people possesses a vast territory, all East Florida and the greatest part of West Florida, which being naturally cut and divided into thousands of islets, knolls, and eminences, by the innumberable rivers, lakes, swamps, vast savannas and ponds, form so many secure retreats and temporary dwelling places, that effectually guard them from any sudden invasions or attacks from their enemies and being such a swampy, hommocky [sic] country, furnishes such a plenty and variety of supplies for the nourishment of varieties of animals, that I can venture to assert, that no part of the globe so abounds with wild game or creatures fit for the food of man.

Thus they enjoy a superabundance of the necessaries and conveniences of life, with the security of person and property, the two great concerns of mankind. The hides of deer, bears, tigers and wolves, together with honey, wax and other productions of the country, purchase their cloathing [sic], equipage and domestic utensils from the whites. They seem to be free from want or desires. No cruel enemy to dread, nothing to give them disquietude, but the gradual encroachments of the white people (Bartram 1958:134).

These quotations from Bartram clearly indicate that in spite of the warfare, disease, and dislocation which all the southeastern tribes suffered, those who were able to re-establish themselves in Florida in the eighteenth century made a successful social adjustment and an adequate ecological adaptation in their new environment. Acquiring some new domesticates from the Spanish, they were able to establish agricultural communities cultivating the new species as well as the traditional crops. They also exploited the wild animals and plant foods in their new location. Indeed, Bartram's description, if taken as an example of average Seminole life, must lead us to believe that Indian life in Florida in the late eighteenth century was little short of idyllic.

After the Creek War of 1813–1814, more Creek Indians moved into Florida, adding to the Muskogee-speaking population while being absorbed into the category "Seminole." Other refugees from the north continued to increase the Florida population from time to time. In fact, three of the Florida towns were occupied by Negroes who settled among them (Swanton 1922:408).

The widespread upheaval in the southeast and the high level of mortality from hostilities and disease produced a situation in which broken political units regrouped to form a single body which absorbed not only Indians, but also renegade whites and Negroes who fled into Spanish Florida to escape slavery.

In 1817–1818 the United States government sent Andrew Jackson into Florida, ostensibly to recover runaway slaves. The result was the First Seminole War, which in turn led, in 1821, to the acquisition of Florida by the United States, for Spain could no longer defend the territory.

At the time Florida was annexed by the United States, the Indian people in that region, all of whom were by then usually referred to as Seminole, occupied farm and pasture land in the heart of the peninsula, as Bartram related. Since the Spanish had not been interested in agriculture and animal husbandry, there had been no conflict between the Spanish and the Indians for land. The Indians had citrus groves and they raised horses and cattle acquired from the Spanish. They were also slave owners, both of black and Indian slaves. Unlike the Spanish, the people of the United States wanted the new land for settlement. A conflict arose. The Treaty of Moultrie Creek, 1823, provided for the removal of the Indians from the choice land to a wilderness farther south in order to settle white farmers and pastoralists on the better land. The Seminole were not strong enough to resist the armed might of the United States so soon after a defeat, and therefore they signed the treaty, although unwillingly. Not a decade had passed, however, before the influx of new settlers created pressure to remove the Seminole once again. This time the plan was to send them to the newly acquired land of the Louisiana Purchase, the area which is now Oklahoma.

A group of Indians agreed to look over the western lands, although they had by this time become content with the provisions of the Treaty of Moultrie Creek. White negotiators claimed that the members of the Indian delegation investigating the western land agreed to accept that territory, but the Seminole remaining in Florida denied that the other Indians had authority to make any agreement that would be binding on all the Florida Indians. Attempts at parley were unsuccessful. Finally, under the leadership of Osceola, the Seminole renewed hostilities with the United States in the Second Seminole War, 1835–1842, which is often referred to as *the* Seminole War since the other two were very much shorter in duration and far less destructive. This war, in which Osceola became the Seminole hero,

> . . . dragged through eight years, not including Jackson's first raid into northern Florida, and . . . cost the United States government, it is estimated, $20,000,000, the lives of many thousand persons of both sexes, and enormous property losses besides (Swanton 1922:412).

Not all Seminoles fought in this war. Some felt that it was not worth another bloody struggle and moved to Oklahoma. Those who refused to go west fled to the south into the everglade and swamp region where it was virtually impossible to flush them out. The Second Seminole War is considered the fiercest of all wars between the United States and the Indians. Osceola was captured under a flag of truce and died in a prison at the age of thirty-four. The other captured Indians were sent west. That group included all of the living Seminole leaders. A census of Florida Indians was taken in 1847. It lists 120 Indian warriors: 70 Seminole, 30 Mikasuki, 12 Creek, 4 Yuchi, and 4 Choctaw (Swanton 1922:28). After the Third Seminole War, 1856–1858, no more than 150 Indians were left in the wild swamp area which no one else wanted.

Of this remaining group, there is no census material to give the linguistic divisions. However, since there are at the present two groups, Mikasuki and Muskogee (which the Indians call Creek), speakers of each language must have remained. It is not known how many of the other Indian people who contributed to the "Seminole" population of earlier years have left descendants among the present Seminole population. Swanton has said that some Calusa existed in their old territory until the end of the last Seminole War (Swanton 1922:27). If that is correct, there is a high probability that there was some intermarriage between the Calusa and Seminole proper in the last half of the nineteenth century. Whatever the elements of the Seminole, certainly it cannot be doubted that in the veins of living people at Big Cypress there must flow the blood from Yuchi, Yamassee, Apalachee, Timucua, and Creek ancestors as well as from the Calusa and others, for all these groups intermarried during the eighteenth and nineteenth centuries.

In 1880 Clay MacCauley of the Bureau of American Ethnology visited the camps of the Seminole of Florida. His study appears in the Fifth Annual Report of the Bureau (1884) and is the first ethnographic work on these people. Unfortunately MacCauley never seemed to realize that he was dealing with two linguistic groups. At the time of his investigation there were five main camp locations scattered through the swamp and everglades: (1) Devil's Garden region, south of Clewiston; (2) Fisheating Creek, flowing into Lake Okeechobee from the west; (3) Catfish Lake, east of Lake Wales; (4) Miami River; and (5) Cow Creek just northeast of Okeechobee City. MacCauley (1884:478) gives the total population as 208.

There was no Mikasuki reservation until the Executive Order of 1911, by which 26,781 acres were set aside. This area, in Hendry County, became the nucleus of Big Cypress Reservation. Although a reservation area had been created, the Indians did not immediately leave their camp sites to settle there. It might be guessed that in 1911 there were no pressures on the Indians to move onto reservation territory. South Florida at that time was a real wilderness. Miami was hardly more than a town, and the big resorts of the coasts had not come into existence. Literally no one but the Indians wanted that desolate land.

> There are no improvements on the Government land held for the Indians in this State. The Indians do not live on it, but make their homes on any spot in the everglades or Cypress Swamp that strikes their fancy (Seminole Indian Agency 1918:1, 2)

Even in 1930 there were numbers of camps off the reservation, and today there are still groups of Indians who prefer not to live on the Indian lands, although since World War II the majority of the Seminole people have established their camps within these areas.

There are three other reservations in Florida today: Brighton (just west of Lake Okeechobee) where most of the Muskogee speakers live; Hollywood (which was called Dania when this fieldwork was started) close to Ft. Lauderdale on the coast; and a new reservation along the Tamiami Trail. In 1965 the Miccosukee Tribe became an incorporated body, distinct from the Seminole Tribe of Florida. The federal agency administering Hollywood, Brighton, and Big Cypress is located at Hollywood, as is the headquarters of the tribal council and board.

Only Brighton has a majority of Muskogee speakers. The inhabitants may move from one reservation to another, but the language groups have remained distinct with most Muskogee speakers staying at Brighton. A few live at Holly-wood, however, in order to be close to agency headquarters. The only Muskogee speakers at Big Cypress are either spouses of Mikasuki or temporary workers.

Big Cypress Reservation is located about 45 miles south of Clewiston and 130 miles by road from Miami. When the access road to the east-west toll road is completed, the distance from the coast (Miami and the agency) will be reduced by about half.

## The Environment

Big Cypress Reservation is located in the northeastern part of Big Cypress Swamp in south Florida. The 42,700 acres of the federal reservation consists of cypress swamp land, prairie, pine and palmetto land, as well as cabbage palm and hard wood hummocks. Of this a total of about 6500 acres had been converted into improved pasture by 1965. In addition to the federal reservation, which is held in trust by the United States government, there is a state reservation of 108,000 acres which abuts on the eastern boundary of the federal reservation and extends into the totally unimproved sawgrass and everglade region. A new toll road runs from Andytown to Naples, cutting across the land of the state reservation.

There are two seasons in southern Florida: wet summers and dry winters. In the late summer the area is often struck by hurricanes from the Caribbean. Without drainage work the prairie areas are almost always under water except during unusually dry winters. The average January temperature for this region is above 65°F. Annual rainfall is in excess of 60 inches, and the growing season averages more than 330 days. The dry period often produces fires which tend to prevent the larger hardwood trees on the hummocks from attaining maturity. Fire also destroys the highly flammable drained peat. For the same reason there is an absence of pines in many areas suitable for their growth. Reforestation has occurred, however, and 80 acres of pine seedlings were hand-planted by the Indians during 1963. Hummocks are low knolls or hillocks, standing higher than the marshland with the appearance of islands during periods of high water. They are moderately to heavily wooded, and sometimes great flocks of white egrets alight in the branches, giving the trees the appearance of being hung with masses of white blossoms. Except for the hummocks, the horizon is utterly flat, a vista of sky and water, broken only by the occasional wooded clumps.

Geologically, Big Cypress Swamp is part of the most recently emerged region of Florida, an area extending from Lake Okeechobee to the southern tip. None of this area is more than 100 feet above sea level. The greatest elevation on the reservation itself is not more than 20 feet above sea level, while the low spot is only 13 feet above that level.

Drainage is only part of the problem at Big Cypress. Because of the dry winters adequate irrigation is also necessary for both the vegetable fields and the improved pastures. Big Cypress is part of the Central and South Florida Flood Control District, and drainage canals have been constructed by the United States

Army Corps of Engineers to control water on the reservation. Completed in 1967, these canals serve two major functions. First, they are expected to lower the water table so that formerly flooded areas are available for agriculture and pasture. In addition, they produce water for irrigation during the dry season. Before the canals had been dug the water for irrigation purposes came from barely adequate wells which could not have been used for any pasture expansion. In terms of development the potentially irrigable area at Big Cypress has been estimated at 11,500 acres.

The soil is sandy, of two distinct types: on the hummocks, a dark mold mixed with marl and clay, and in the swamp, muck and peat which when properly drained is very rich. With supplements of complete fertilizer this land is excellent for intensive winter cultivation of vegetables for northern markets. It is also good land for the improved pasture grasses such as Pensacola Bahia and Pangola with clover. The rest of the soil is made up of a light, shallow sandy cover over underlying limestone. When this soil cover is deep enough for grass roots, it can be fertilized and used for pasture.

Roy Nash, who made a survey of the Florida Seminole in 1930, described the area previous to changes in the landscape resulting from modern technology.

. . . Big Cypress is waste and water. A wilderness where cypress heads, clumps of slash pine, and occasional high hammocks vary the monotony of open prairies. The saw palmetto is abundant; soil is not. Limestone outcrops over much of the region.

Most of the Big Cypress is so flooded in the wet season as to be impenetrable except to a man on foot or by ox team. The Indians shove their canoes along the

*The swamp environment.*

*Framework for the traditional Chickee.*

eastern margin when the water is high. In the driest part of the dry season the Cypress can be traversed in a Ford.

That is, if one knows his crossings. For Okaloacoochee Slough traverses the Cypress from north to south, and Okaloacoochee is treacherous always. A bog 60 miles long. If the Big Cypress is desolation, Okaloacoochee is the depth of despair. Between Okaloacoochee and the Everglades the bulk of the Seminoles have their homes (Nash 1931:15).

*A CBS (cement block structure) house—there are ten on the reservation.*

*Washing the laundry in a drainage canal.*

The Indians no longer travel by canoe, but the description still fits most of Big Cypress today.

Most dwellings are still very similar to the traditional *chickee* described by MacCauley in 1880 with the exception that nails are used in place of lashing and some milled lumber is used for the platforms. Previously these dwellings were built on the higher ground, but with increasingly extensive and efficient drainage, it is becoming more common to use lower lying areas and to build the camps closer together. However, these lower areas must still often be abandoned during the hurricanes. Because of the similarity to contemporary dwellings, MacCauley's (1884:500) description is a useful one:

> . . . approximately 16 by 9 feet in ground measurement, made almost altogether, if not wholly, of materials taken from the palmetto tree. It is actually but a platform elevated about three feet from the ground and covered with a palmetto thatched roof, the roof being not more than 12 feet above the ground at the ridge pole, or seven at the eaves. Eight upright palmetto logs, unsplit and undressed, support the roof. Many rafters sustain the palmetto thatching. The platform is composed of split palmetto logs lying transversely, flat side up, upon beams which extend the length of the building and are lashed to the uprights by palmetto ropes, thongs, or trader's ropes. This platform is peculiar, in that it fills the interior of the building like a floor and serves to furnish the family with a dry sitting or lying down place when, as often happens, the whole region is under water . . .

The Seminole's house is open on all sides without rooms. It is, in fact, only a covered platform.

Today there are ten units of cement block structures, called CBS, a type of housing approved by the state as "hurricane proof." These structures were built in 1960 and are occupied by nuclear or extended families, one member of which owns cattle. Only someone who owns cattle may own a house because cattle are the security of the house mortgage. The houses are wired for electricity, which was put through to the reservation under a rural electrification program at the time the houses were built. A number of chickees have electricity now too. Until 1967 there were no phones at Big Cypress, and the only means of communication with the outside was a two-way radio to Hollywood, the reservation headquarters.

The cement block structures contain either two or three bedrooms and modern bathrooms and kitchens. They were built in a cluster and have their own deep well water system, whereas each individual chickee owner must sink his own well if he desires one. The new structures are also on a sewage system. On the other hand, only one chickee has a flush toilet latrine with a septic tank; the rest either have privies or nothing at all. Water pollution is therefore a problem. Several of the houses have washing machines in a small outside utility storeroom. People in the chickees usually wash their laundry in the canals or in wash tubs, rinsing the clothes in the canals, or go to laundromats in town.

The CBS are sturdily built with modern conveniences, and in general the owners have enjoyed the comforts and conveniences they offer.

I didn't like the house at first. When I looked around all I could see were walls and there seemed to be no place to sit down. We didn't have a washing machine at first so we washed clothes in the bathtub. But I liked the kitchen.

However, there are drawbacks to life in a CBS, one being the greater summer heat inside compared to the traditional chickee which is open on all sides to catch the breezes. Another big drawback for many is the expense. Acknowledging these problems, the housing branch of the agency started a self-help home building program in 1967. Professional craftsmen put in the electric and plumbing systems, but the rest of the construction was done by men of the community on a reciprocal basis under the direction of the housing branch. Plans have been made for each camp to have three separate units: one for living and sleeping quarters; one for cooking and dining; and one for a bathroom with shower, toilet, and sink. The kitchen unit will have an electric stove, modern sink with cabinets, and a refrigerator.

The units are wooden, raised on a poured cement base, and almost continuous window areas circle each unit at a height of about 4 feet. The windows are screened, and can be closed in cool weather. This new housing combines the advantages of free-air flow which makes the chickee so appealing during the hot weather, with the CBS advantages of a dry, easy to clean floor, screening, and modern electrical facilities and plumbing. The cost is low and largely covered by a government grant. When I was at Big Cypress in 1968, no camp had all the

*An example of the new self-help housing.*

units completely finished, but there was obvious enthusiasm for the whole idea. It remains to be seen how the units will hold up during a hurricane.

The owners of the houses consider that they own a lot on which the houses stand, and they have stakes marking out the boundaries unless these happen to have decayed. People in the chickees do not think of owning land. Instead, they speak of owning the pumps and the wells, giving as a reason the fact that they paid for drilling and installation. However, they do not consider that the land belongs to them as individuals. The camps are usually traditional sites in the sense that people now represent second or third generations on the site, but it is the camp and buildings, not the land, which they conceive of as theirs. Even the people in the cement block houses do not own the property in the sense that they have complete control of its disposal. They cannot sell it to anyone, although their heirs may inherit it. In case of nonpayment of mortgage charges, the property reverts to the tribe.

## The Subsistence Basis

In 1955 a program of renting land to commercial vegetable growers was initiated whereby the growers agreed to lease the land, develop it, ditch and drain it, raise vegetables for two years, and then turn it back to the tribe sodded or seeded in the improved grasses. Although this plan has proven satisfactory, there is greater demand for improved pastures than the commercial growers can supply. Therefore the Bureau of Indian Affairs has extended funds to assist with land and pasture development. By 1966 approximately 6500 acres had been planted with improved pasture grasses, Bahia Pensacola and Pangola, and various legumes.

All intensive agriculture on the reservation is carried out by the large-scale commercial growers who lease the land from the tribe. Their main market is the northern consumer in the winter. Thus, although they maintain a year-round operation, it slackens off in the summer. The Indians show no interest in cultivating the soil because of the recent accessibility of grocery stores, and because the interest in cattle has forced the use of good land for pasture. Another reason may be that since the land is tribally owned, individuals have no claim on acreage large enough for sizable farming operations. Indeed, there are no legal provisions for individual use of land beyond the area immediately surrounding a camp site where most Indians have kitchen gardens. However, there is not enough produce from these gardens, nor is it of high enough quality, to supply an income from marketing. Such agricultural products as cane syrup, mentioned by Nash, are no longer manufactured and sold by Indians.

During the winter when the commercial vegetable growers are at the peak of their activity, almost any man or woman who wishes may get a job at $7.50 a day for field labor or $10.00 a day for driving a tractor (1965). Employment is available on the ranches leased on the reservation as well as on the ranches and plantations in the surrounding area. The income derived from such agricultural activity is seasonal, and the season is not long enough for most workers to earn enough to last out the year without additional income or government contributions of surplus food. By contrast, a few jobs do last the year round, but they are usually filled by Mexicans, Puerto Ricans, or Negroes who live in the area. No Indian really likes agricultural harvesting when it involves hand labor, although driving farm machinery is acceptable as permanent work.

Although the Mikasuki do not obtain a livelihood from farming, almost every camp has some cultivated plants around it. The gardens are little better than wild in most cases, and only a small part of the vegetable diet is home-grown. Even corn products are frequently purchased at the store. However, most camps have a clump of sugar cane, some corn, and a sweet potato vine or two. Some gardens also contain sour oranges and banana trees, white lemons, beans, custard apples, pineapple, water melons, cabbage, guavas, mangoes, and pumpkins are cultivated by a few families. Only two camps have really well-cared-for gardens, and those are camps occupied by very old people. The rest are largely untended.

Although not as abundant as they once were, game, fish, and fowl are still so plentiful that they are the major source of protein. Deer is the primary object of the hunt, with venison being the main wild meat eaten. Deer are still easy to find. The Indians eat a number of wild bird and fish species, and turtles are an especially relished item in the diet.

At one time otter pelts were an important source of cash, but the disappearance of the otter has put an end to this income. Three of the four poisonous snakes found in North America are among the reptile fauna of Big Cypress: the coral snake, the rattlesnake, and the water moccasin. Only the copperhead is not found there. However, the Indians do not eat any of the snakes. An occasional alligator is still killed. The meat of the tail is sometimes eaten and the hide sold. Whether or not this is illegal is a moot point; the government claims alligators and certain other species are in danger of becoming extinct and has protected them by law. The Indians, on the other hand, claim they have the right to kill any game except the plumed egret within the boundaries of the reservation.

In terms of forest products Big Cypress has the following trees: slash pine, cabbage palm, pond cypress, and live oak. These lumber resources have not yet been exploited to any great degree although dead-heart cypress fence posts yield a regular but small income for a few members of the tribe. The tribe also sells cabbage palm spikes for Palm Sunday church services. Contracts are given to commercial lumber interests to cut trees, but the income from lumber is erratic. Noncommercial use of timber includes palm fronds for thatching roofs, swamp cabbage for food, dead tree trunks for chickee posts, and palmetto fiber for the bodies of the dolls that the women make for sale at the Arts and Crafts Center on the coast at Dania.

Prior to 1955 cattle belonging to Indians grazed on native pastures, a term indicating unimproved grasslands, which were partially under water and produced less nutritive grasses. The results were uneconomical, the calf crop produced being a mere 20 percent as compared to 60 percent when pasture land is improved. Local experts hope that future calf crops will average better than 80 percent as improvements in management land use practices recommended by the state university continue to be adopted by the cattle owners.

With the elimination of native range under the commercial growers' program, a better breed of cattle can be pastured, and it is expected that the product will be competitive with cattle raised among the general Florida population. Native range is capable of supporting no better breeds than Spanish-scrub cattle, or a cross between that variety and the water-tolerant Brahman. Only varieties of the quality of Angus or Hereford will be competitive on the beef markets.

On native range with a Brahma-scrub cross breed, the beef yield was only about nine pounds an acre per year. The local agricultural experiment station of the University of Florida has been able to produce a yield of 810 pounds of beef per acre on improved land with an improved breed.

In 1968 no one at Big Cypress was receiving enough cash from cattle to make stock raising his only source of income. Two hundred head were considered the economic unit by agronomist experts by which is meant that a calf crop of 80 percent on a herd that size would bring in sufficient money after costs so that other income would be unnecessary. No one had 200 head then, and no one was getting an 80 percent calf crop. The cattle-program planning has been toward the goal that all capable stock owners would eventually have an economic unit in cattle and therefore an assured income. The goal is still to be achieved.

Insect control has improved markedly with the use of insecticides and natural predators of insect life. A species of wading bird, called by the Indians the cattle egret, was imported some years ago to inhabit the pastures and eat the insects stirred up by the grazing cattle. The worst time of the year for cattle is the summer when the heat is very great and the humidity high. At that time annoying insects may cause the animals to walk all day and night in order to gain some relief from the biting. The constant activity causes a loss of weight just before market time in the late summer. However, insect control gets better every year, and destructive parasites like the screw worm have been entirely eliminated. Mosquito abatement has been moderately successful, especially around the camps. Mosquitoes are rare around the homes during the day, and the yellow fever carrier, *Aedes aegypti*, is not found in the area. At night, though, everyone uses mosquito netting where there are no screens for protection. The mosquitoes too are at their worst during the humid summers. Nevertheless, the present situation is a great improvement over that which Nash (1931:17, 18) found in 1930 when he wrote: "The rattlesnake is a housepet compared with sand flies, horseflies or mosquitoes."

Hogs, a popular livestock during the early part of this century, have all but disappeared. The medicine men are traditionally expected to be paid in stock, and one "doctor" still has quite a few pigs. At present he is the only hog raiser on the reservation, and he does not own any cattle. About half of the camps have a few chickens in pens or running about, but chicken is just as frequently purchased from grocery stores.

As recently as the 1950s some Indian men made enough money frog hunting to support their families. Frog legs are a gourmet delicacy in coastal restaurants, and frog hunters used to take their wives and children with them out into the swamp-everglade wilderness where they made camp on a hummock. From this base camp the father and any other older males in the group went out by air boat or in earlier times by dugout canoe to hunt, leaving the women and children at their temporary home. Then the catch was taken to the city and sold. By the 1960s frog hunting was no longer an important source of income.

Both men and women work at crafts, making such items as gaily colored garments, dolls, basketry, carvings, etc. A diligent craftsman can make $1000.00 a year from the sale of these objects to tourists through the Arts and Crafts Center at Hollywood or through the various private tourist attractions in south Florida. Few people make this much, however, although in some cases the income probably makes the difference between having luxury items such as electric appliances and doing without. Craft work is no longer seasonal to the degree that agriculture is, for more and more tourists are going to Florida for summer vacations. There have been some men who sew, but most of the male craftsmen are wood carvers who work at crafts only as temporary employment in the agricultural off-season. The women workers most frequently are wives who are not otherwise employed. The women sew almost all the family clothes and the craft sewing is almost a continuation of family work. Since electrification, most of the families have electric sewing machines, but there are still a few women who do all their sewing on the hand-cranked, mechanical model.

In 1965, out of a total population of 259, there were seven welfare recipients and six social security recipients at Big Cypress. There had been two other men on welfare, but they had been eliminated from the program when they obtained cattle loans, even though the cattle had not brought in any cash.

*Seminole arts and crafts. Two styles of Sofki spoons (top). Drawstring purses (below). Some are crafted with cloth bottoms and others with basketry bottoms of palmetto fiber and swamp grass. These and other items are sold at the Arts and Crafts Center.*

*Old man displaying the Sofki spoons he carved for the author.*

Understandably the Indians did not comprehend why this should be, and the result was a situation frought with antagonism and suspicion. The federal agency has no control over welfare, which is handled by the county, and even though the agency personnel made an official protest when these old people were cut off, it was to no avail. In the eyes of the Indians, there is no difference in the various levels of government, and they do not discriminate between the county and the Bureau of Indian Affairs. This is an example of why the Indians think the agency officials are so unpredictable. First they gave the Indians welfare funds, then they cut off the funds because the Indians had a cattle loan. The Indian men involved in this situation never received cash from the cattle sales, but the mere fact of the loan was enough to stop their welfare checks. Agency behavior is mystifying to the Indians, who expected to have more income when they bought cattle, but in fact ended up with less.

Five men have been employed by the federal government in land operations and road work, two by the state, and one by the county. In 1965 the salaries for these men ranged from $3420.00 per year for the county worker to $5260.00 for the emyployee of the branch of land operations. There have also been five tribal employees whose salary range is $200.00 to $4420.00 per year. Those who earn the largest salary in each category have also been elected officials of the reservations and, in addition, have been the president and vice president of the Cattlemen's Association.

The income per family in 1964 is given in Table 1.

TABLE 1
INCOME PER FAMILY UNIT 1964

| Income | Number of Families | Percent |
|---|---|---|
| 5000–7999 | 5 | 10.2 |
| 3000–4999 | 11 | 22.5 |
| 2000–2999 | 9 | 18.3 |
| 1000–1999 | 13 | 26.5 |
| under 1000 | 7 | 14.3 |
| unknown | 4 | 8.1 |

These figures were released by the agency May 19, 1965, and are based upon 49 resident families and a population of 259. The highest individual family income in 1964 was $7070.46. The average family contained 4.1 individuals, and there are a few old people living alone who do not belong to any family unit.

With the exception of salaried employees of the government or the tribe, it is impossible to state with precision what the individual incomes are. Many people are paid cash for goods or services without resort to social security or income tax statements. The Indians themselves, being illiterate, keep no records. Employment is sporadic and seasonal, and for almost every family there is more than one worker. All of this, combined with the lack of records, make the accuracy of the statistics doubtful. However, one thing is certain, the average Indian family income is far below the average non-Indian income in Florida, and it is conceded that the Indians are generally underemployed. If the climate were worse, or if wild foods were less plentiful, many of Big Cypress would be in real need at one time or another.

When I first lived at Big Cypress, I often heard people mention the possibility of storekeeping as a desirable form of employment. It was the custom for some people to sell soft drinks at their camps, and three people had a small inventory of packaged staples for sale as well as the cold drinks. However, income derived from these sales was negligible. The sales were a matter more of convenience than business enterprise. The market at Big Cypress being very limited, it never was at all likely that any large outfit would be interested in opening up a local store. And, of course, no private store owner could be successful either. However, the tribe decided to build and operate a store through the tribal enterprises. In early 1967 it was opened for business, and about nine months later a gasoline pump was installed in front of the store. On sale were complete lines of canned and packaged foods, as well as dairy products, fresh vegetables, and frozen meats. Also various sundries such as bolts of yard goods, flash lights, toiletries, and fishing supplies were available.

The store itself was built of cement blocks and was air-conditioned. Non-Indian workers on the canal project and on the leased farms were patrons as well as the Indians. The store has been well received by the Big Cypress population, and at this time it appears to be, if not a financial success, at least not losing money. The children especially have enjoyed the opportunity to buy ice-cream cones, popsicles, cold drinks, candies, and other delights. Before the store was built, shopping meant a 45 mile trip to Clewiston or an almost equally long trip to Immokalee.

The first manager of the store was an Indian woman who had been the first Big Cypress girl to graduate from the public school in Clewiston (Garbarino 1970). She had gone to business college after high school and then had worked for three years in a Miami bank. When the job of manager was offered to her, she decided to take it in spite of the fact that she liked her work at the bank very much and was quite content living in Miami. I had known her when she lived in the city, and she had once remarked to me that she liked living in the city so much that she did not think she could ever go back to live permanently on the reservation. I was, therefore, quite surprised when she wrote to me of her decision to return. It was, she said, because she wanted to use her education to help her people. If she had refused to take the position, a white person would have been hired, for there was no other Indian with the required training in bookkeeping. In addition to the manager, there was a second sales person, another woman, and they were assisted in menial chores by teenagers employed under provisions of the Neighborhood Youth Corps program.

In the fall of 1966 the recreation hall was converted into a woodcraft shop in an attempt to provide employment on the reservation. High power woodworking equipment was installed, and both men and women responded with some enthusiasm. That enthusiasm was short-lived, however, for problems soon arose between the Indian manager and the employees about keeping regular hours. The employees needed a strong manager to control the quality and quantity of the output, and the manager was under pressure from the agency to observe the hours and productivity standard in industry. The Indians preferred piecework conditions. Both men and women held the managerial position for short times, and both were equally unsuccessful because there was a conflict between traditional attitudes toward work and the wage-labor expectations of the agency personnel. Managers found the contention too disagreeable to endure. They quit rather than "boss" people around. The employees preferred working at their own pace, as they were accustomed to do with their traditional crafts. The shop was closed about a year and a half after it opened.

Programs of the Office of Economic Opportunity have been more successful in creating jobs on the reservation. There is a Headstart School, employing young women as full-time teaching aids, and a nursery school which not only employs mothers, but also provides day care for children of mothers who work elsewhere. A hot lunch is provided for the children in both schools, and more women are employed in kitchen work.

The Community Action Program created a position for a social worker's aide on the reservation. This particular job, like the managerial position at the woodworking shop, has been hard to keep filled. Both men and women have tried it, but their tenure has been short. Difficulties appear to have arisen between the Indian aide and the white administrative hierarchy and also between the aide and other Indians. At this writing, it appears that if the position continues to be funded through O.E.O., it will gradually begin to function as it was intended, that is, to increase interaction and information between the social worker and the Indian population and to bring increased benefits to the Indians. However, it will require a longer period of adjustment because it is a role which is too new to be accepted rapidly by the Indian people and too exacting to be handled competently by any individual without previous experience.

There are various jobs which the Neighborhood Youth Corps program has opened for teenagers who until this opportunity had almost no chance for steady income. As with the other programs, there has been conflict between the hour and work expectation of the dominant society and the traditions of the Indian people, but in general the young people have been well pleased to have the work.

Although viewing television has introduced the Indians to a wider range of occupations than they would otherwise be aware of, this knowledge does not seem to have changed anyone's hopes for future employment. Concepts of jobs other than agricultural labor are limited to the sort of wage work which some few have done in the past, in particular, heavy equipment operation. Three young men said that they would really prefer operating road building machinery to anything else. One boy said he wanted to be a teacher, but very few young people, with the exception of two who wanted to be auto mechanics, had any definite ideas about employment which they might enjoy. The attitude is perhaps a result of viewing work as necessary in order to get money to buy desired things rather than seeing work as a commitment or career.

I'd like a job here on the reservation. No, I don't have any job in mind. There are lots of things I'd like to have, but I don't have any money. I'd like a car.

I don't want to work regular. Seems like that's not much of a life. I'd just work to buy things and then quit.

A job is good for income, but I don't like people telling me what to do. I like to do something when I feel like it.

The boy who wanted to be a social science teacher said that he was very glad to have a job with the Neighborhood Youth Corps.

I can make some money in the summer when there is no school. I would like to go to college some day, and that takes lots of money, so I better start getting some now.

I asked the Indian in charge of Headstart for her opinion about the difference between working mothers and Neighborhood Youth Corps teenage employees.

The kids goof off all the time. They resent me. The mothers were a little bit slow at first, but then they worked real well. They value their jobs because they can use the money and experience to help their children. The Neighborhood Youth Corps kids are irresponsible. They like to have money, but they don't have a goal to save for. They spend it on beer for a week-end. They don't care much one way or the other. It is not good to have money without control. I think there is less gas sniffing but much more teenage drinking. All the women who drink are teen-agers. None of the older women with families drink, even though many of their husbands do. The men go out and drink alone, and then they give the younger girls something to drink and start messing around, the older men and younger girls. The mothers are more responsible. They have to think about their children because the men don't.

Some Big Cypress people have gone to Hollywood reservation to work at Amphenol, an electronic components plant which was opened there in 1967 to tap the Indian labor supply. Amphenol and other companies have established manufacturing units on a number of reservations as part of the Industrial Development Program of the Bureau of Indian Affairs. The program encourages private industrial enterprises to open branches on or near reservations in order to increase employment opportunities for Indians. Although reaching only a small percentage of the unemployed and underemployed Indians, the program is generally considered successful. The importance of the plan lies in the fact that Indians do not have to leave their homes to find work. However, for the Big Cypress Indians, the distance to Hollywood is too great for commuting so they must move to the Hollywood Reservation if they want jobs at Amphenol.

Some of the Big Cypress people have done just that, but for most the length of stay has been very short. English-speaking ability is a necessity for employment at Amphenol, and that rules out many people from Big Cypress. Nevertheless, some of the residents have moved to Hollywood to take a job at the plant. Indians from Hollywood and Brighton also work there. Since the plant opened in 1967, more than 70 Indians have been employed. In September 1968, fewer than 20 were still working there, non-Indians having replaced the others. The program is still too new to conclude that it is a failure, but the already discussed conflict between differing wage-labor expectations has apparently played an important part in the high dropout rate at Amphenol. Several Big Cypress people I talked to also mentioned the amount of drinking at Hollywood which they found distasteful. Some young people who have gone to live at Hollywood to work at Amphenol have worried their parents who fear that the exposure to the more sophisticated Hollywood life will corrupt them. When young people living at Hollywood begin to drink, the parents blame the Hollywood environment and bad companions rather than their children.

I was told that a knitting mill near Hollywood had experimented with Indian women employees for a while, but the women who started there proved to be so unsatisfactory that the owners refused to hire any more Indians. The Indian who told me about that incident said that the employer was displeased with the absenteeism and tardiness, and she added, "A few Indian women destroyed an opportunity for all the others." In her opinion the tribal leaders were at fault because they always found excuses if Indians did not work up to standard.

> They just make excuses. They don't tell the people they are wrong. Then the leaders find some temporary work for the ones who quit or get government aid for them. That is bad. I say don't give them aid if they get fired. Make them responsible. It is lack of responsibility that is the root of the problem. There are too many handouts and too much coddling. It's not a question of training but a question of responsibility.

The respondent had been successfully employed for a number of years both on and off the reservation. She said, "No one made excuses for me. I told myself I had to do it. It was hard, but I did it."

I asked another person who had a good work record why some people worked well and stayed on the job while others did not.

> Some want nice things, lots of appliances and a good home. Some have been trained by their parents to accept responsibility. Other people never had any responsibility at home and their parents were not responsible either, lazy hunters and things like that. But they spoil it for the others. They would rather have an easy, lazy life with not much money and things than to have a hard life with good income. People have to decide for themselves, but it's too bad that employers only remember the ones who don't work.

# 3

# Life at Big Cypress

## The Field Situation

DURING MY FIRST FOUR MONTHS at Big Cypress I lived in a household composed entirely of women and girls. Head of the household was a woman of about forty, and living with her were her brother's two daughters. One of these girls, though only in her teens, had two little girls. Her husband was in jail, and that meant there was room for me to join the household. It was convenient for me, a woman, and fortunate, too, because the all-woman household made our mutual adjustment easier and faster than it probably would have been otherwise. By the next year, when I lived with a family of husband, wife, and daughter, I was used to Big Cypress, and the residents appeared to have become used to my presence also.

Ellie, the head of the household where I first lived, was very kind and thoughtful. She did everything possible to make me comfortable, and even wanted to cook my meals for me. I did eat with the family quite often, but not regularly, for Ellie was a tractor driver at that time, and was at work during the day. When she returned home, she was tired, and I did not wish to burden her with my meals. Therefore, except on week-ends and for special occasions, I ate canned foods which I brought in from Clewiston every other week.

There are three unusual items of the Seminole diet which should be mentioned: sofki, fry bread, and swamp cabbage. Sofki is the traditional Seminole drink. It is usually made from corn which has been mashed or pounded, then boiled until it becomes a thin cream. Sofki can be made with vegetables other than corn, for instance pumpkin or tomatoes, but corn is the most common form. Outsiders do not find sofki very tasty. It is like a thin gruel with lumps. However, Seminole people old and young like it very much and drink it in preference to milk or water with meals. Fry bread is made by almost all Indians of the United States. The Seminole variety is much like that of other areas, made of flour, salt, leavening, and shortening, and fried in deep fat in a frying pan. It is like a large biscuit, fried instead of baked. Swamp cabbage, called "hearts of palm" by outsiders, is the inner part of the sabal palm. In Florida it is considered quite a delicacy. It can be eaten both cooked and raw.

Ellie's niece, Jannie, the mother of the two babies, worked sporadically as jobs became available. One of the pastures was being sodded with good grazing grasses, and when the sods came in by truck, there was an immediate demand for field labor to get the sod laid. At those times, Jannie would work twelve to fifteen hours without stopping except for meals. Then perhaps for a week or more she would be at home with no wage work, although she usually busied herself with doll-making, which was also Ellie's evening occupation.

Jannie seemed to like having me there. She was curious about many things, and by the end of the first month of my stay, she began to sit by my side in the evening while I worked over my notes. We talked about anything and everything, often turning off all lights to keep the heat down as much as possible. Frequently Ellie and Liza joined us, and our bilingual discussion ranged far and wide, with Ellie and Jannie conferring to figure out how to explain something to me in a combination of Mikasuki and English. It never seemed to bother them at all that I wrote down what was said. As a matter of fact, after I had become an established member of the household, one of the women might suggest that she had thought of something I should take down in the notebook.

At first my presence in the household made Liza shy, but she enjoyed watching me type up my notes. She sat by my side, virtually for hours, without moving, just watching me. She had seen typewriters at school, but it was a new experience to have one in her own home. I let her type on it after awhile. She could speak and understand English, but she was very bashful about it at first. I taught her to sing "Frère Jacques" which she called the French song. I tried to teach her "Zwei Herzen in drei Viertel Toch," but she never quite mastered that one.

Liza was only ten years old. Her ability to care for the two babies in the family astonished me. She did more than keep them amused while the older women worked. She fed them and bathed them with adult competence. However, if both women expected to be away for a whole day or longer, all three children were taken to the camp of a relative who had many children of her own, and who always found room for children of working mothers. Women always helped each other out in this fashion even when not related, although it was most common to go first to a relative. Little girls also were expected to care for younger siblings, and the oldest girl in a family often spent her childhood helping raise her younger brothers and sisters rather than at play. Little girls we would consider mere children seemed so competent handling babies that it was hard to realize how young they really were. At the same time, these little girls often were left with tremendous responsibility for which they were not really prepared, and frequently they had no one around whom they could count on in an emergency. It sometimes seemed to me that Liza had had no childhood. One older woman recounting her experience said to me,

Myself, I went through that. My mother had to work, and I was the one to baby-sit for my aunts' and sisters children and my little brother. I mean that was expected of me. So I just carried on, and now I feel as though I never did really have a childhood of my own to enjoy. I feel as though I just grew up too fast. I started around nine, and I was really working then. Most of the parents here expect that. But today's teenagers don't want to do that so I think that is one thing kids have against parents today. So they just get angry and take off. But Headstart helps the working mothers and some teenage girls work in Headstart and get paid, and they enjoy doing that, but they don't want responsibility, only on their own time and for pay. But it wasn't like that when I was little.

After the Headstart and Community Action projects were begun in the midsixties, the working mothers had an organized program for day care of children. The Community Action Program also employed some mothers to care for the children as well as employing some teenagers as aides. All the Indians were under the supervision of a director who gave them instructions in many phases of child care, and thus increased their chances of gainful employment as well as knowledge of sanitation and good dietary practices. The women so employed had never had a chance for wage work in which they could be with their children. But in the years before the community program, mutual self-help and reliance on older children were the only solutions to day care for little children.

Early one Sunday morning, before the heat and humidity were unbearable, Ellie asked if I would like to see where she drove her tractor. Ellie, the two babies, Jannie, Liza, and I piled into my car and drove down the marl-bedded road. Since it had not rained recently, the roads were dry and traction was good. When it has been raining, marl becomes very slippery and sticky. It becomes encrusted on the underparts of cars and is very difficult to remove once it has hardened, for it forms a coating very like limey cement. Marl is composed of sand, clay, and disintegrating limey remains of prehistoric shell fish. When it is not wet, it makes a good road surface through the swampy areas, piled high above the ground water level and properly graded. A few of the Indian men have good-paying jobs keeping the marl roads graded properly. Their work, done with heavy road equipment, is never really done because there is always the danger that the high water levels will undermine the roadways. Underneath the marl lies the rich organic peaty deposits known as "muck," sadly sticky if a car becomes mired in it, but so fertile that it is mined and sold for top soil.

That day the road was dry and the sky filled with high billowing clouds set off by the contrast to the utter flatness of the land below. That flatness and vast horizon always reminded me of the desert southwest, although as far as humidity and vegetation go, there are hardly two environments less alike. I remarked several times on the beauty of the clouds over the swamp, and said that I found the storm clouds exciting when they came up, as they did so frequently in summer, all of a sudden, coming from nowhere to overwhelm the world. I had never seen such towering clouds. Finally Ellie said something in Mikasuki which I did not understand, and Jannie translated, "She wants to know what kind of clouds you have where you live." I tried to explain how skyscrapers and deciduous trees cut off the expanse of the sky, but they had never seen a city like Chicago, and I could not make them understand.

Suddenly Ellie asked me to stop. To my surprise she jumped from my car, gathered up her long skirt, and waded into the canal which ran beside the road. I must have looked as startled as I felt because Jannie and Liza laughed hard, but they explained that Ellie had seen a turtle and wanted it for soup. Sure enough, Ellie climbed up the banks of the canal, smiling in victory with what seemed to me an incredibly large turtle. She was still holding up her skirts while holding the turtle, which was paddling wildly in the air. I later saw larger turtles than that one, but on that morning it appeared to me a veritable monster. They put the turtle in the trunk of the car, and we started off again, the turtle making me feel most uncomfortable for the rest of the ride by its constant banging around trying to get out. None of my companions appeared concerned with the animal's probable discomfort in the airless enclosure as the day grew hotter and hotter. Very few of the Big Cypress people thought of animals in terms of "pets," but I had had a pet turtle once.

We bounced over the rutted roads, and Ellie eventually indicated a gate in the wire fence which surrounds all the pastures. She got out and opened it. Then we drove into the pasture itself. There were no cattle grazing in the area at that time, because the grass was only a foot high. It would have to grow to a height of about four feet before the cattle would be let back in to feed. The ground was no longer hard marl, but rather soft soil into which I could feel the car wheels sinking. I was worried as I had already been stuck in the soft dirt. The car was loaded rather heavily, so I suggested we turn back. Ellie had wanted to show me where she worked. She was proud of her job. It paid $10.00 a day. This was good pay for women. Most of them could not drive a tractor and therefore earned only $7.50 as field workers. They planted the pasture sods by hand, a back-breaking job, and definitely not so prestigeous as tractor driving. But one part of the pasture looks like any other part, and Ellie, happy that I had visited the scene of her labor, directed me back to the gate to my great relief. Had we become bogged down in the field it would have been serious. We were three or four miles from any camp and by that time of day the heat was fierce. There is no shade in the pasture during the day which makes the women's daily work there even more grueling, and explains why the women would just as soon do some work at night.

As we locked the gate behind us, I noticed a large snake in the drainage ditch. The women told me it was not the poisonous water moccasin but a harmless relative. I remembered Ellie plunging into the canal to get the turtle. She could not possibly have had time to look for moccasins, or cotton mouths, as they are often called. I said as much, but the women assured me that they could spot a dangerous snake very quickly, and that they learned from childhood to be on the lookout for them. The coral snake whose bite is very poisonous has become rare, but the ditches and canals abound with moccasins, and rattlesnakes are not infrequently found in the pasturelands. I remember two cases of snakebite, one serious enough to require a hospital stay, but in general the snakes stay away from the camp and house areas.

Back in the car we continued our tour of the reservation. The unusually dry (for that time of year) land allowed us to visit some abandoned camps whose owners had moved closer to the school, clinic, and agency radio building. The clustering of camps and the ten new cement block buildings now form a nucleus which is a center of population concentration. However, the old camp sites are still remembered and the past inhabitants are still considered owners. "That's so-and-so's old camp," they say.

There are two roads around the reservation open to car travel. One is called the north boundary road, and the other the south boundary. In recent years a third road has been planned to join with the east-west toll road called Alligator Alley. The access road to Alligator Alley had just been completed the last time I visited Big Cypress (summer 1970). It will shorten the trip from the reservation to the coast by nearly one-half. Before the construction of the toll road, to get to the agency at Hollywood on the coast, it was necessary to drive to Clewiston (over a road which only in the late fifties was paved), down US 27. The trip to go almost due east, therefore, used to require a detour almost fifty miles north in order to reach a paved southbound road.

The north boundary road leads to the highest elevation on the reservation, 21 feet above sea level. It passes an area that was planted in 1963 with slash pine, which the Indians hope will grow to commercial timber. Often one sees deer bounding across this road. The deer are small compared to northern species. To the Indians, deer are still an important source of meat. Also along the road, where one rarely meets any people, there are many tropical birds. Egrets are the most common but the anhinga (which the Indians call water turkey) is also seen, as is the rare blue heron and numerous hawks and owls high in the cypress trees. There are also the inevitable unpleasant buzzards, or vultures, going about their scavaging business in a repulsive sort of way but, nevertheless, performing a necessary job.

Meanwhile, getting back to the journey in question, the heat intensified. Jannie suggested that we go to one of the camps and buy a cold drink. In the days before the store was built the soft-drink distributor sent a truck to Big Cypress once a week. It was customary for the families to buy several cases of carbonated drinks. Since electric lines had been run to the reservation, many camps and all the CBS had refrigeration. Those people who had a large refrigeration capacity sold chilled soft drinks and very often a few staples such as bread and canned soup. When the sales took place in a chickee separate from living quarters, it was referred to as a store.

At the first two camps we visited we were told that the cold drink supply was exhausted because it was the end of the week and delivery was the next day. At the third stop we were in luck. It was one of the "stores" and there were still some drinks left. The Big Cypress people consume a large volume of soft drinks, not only because of the heat, but also because the water is sulphur water, which is not very palatable even to the residents who are used to it. Frequently Indians who have been living off the reservation will bring their own water supply in five-gallon jugs when they come back to visit. The sulphur also leaves ugly stains in the sinks, toilets, and bath tubs in the dwellings that have those fixtures.

We sat in the camp and drank the cold beverages from the bottles. That camp had a TV set, and the children and most of the adults were watching it.

TV was still not common on the reservation. When the Rural Electrification Administration put in electricity, the tribe had installed a TV set in the recreation hall, but there was vandalism, or at least mistreatment, to the degree that the set was out of order more often than it was in working condition. The tribal government had the set removed. A few people bought TV for their camps or homes shortly after the electricity was available. One of the elected officials had a color TV set. It was the first time I had ever seen color TV. It was generally believed by the Indians, and it was probably a correct belief, that the children were aided in learning English by having a TV set. One little girl in whose camp I lived used to sing a number of commercials in English before she had been to school. Neither of her parents spoke English. Although her English vocabulary was strangely skewed, she seemed much more at ease with her second language than did her little cousin who was without TV.

Dark clouds began to pile up in the sky indicating that the afternoon storm was approaching. Summer storms are fierce and frightening at Big Cypress, with great flashes of lightning and blasts of thunder accompanied by torrents of rain. When the West Indies hurricanes reach Big Cypress, the result is unbelievable. I was there in 1965 when hurricane Cleo struck. It defies my descriptive powers to communicate that experience. We left the camp and started back home.

The storm proved to be a false alarm. It stayed to the south, over the Everglades leaving the Big Cypress area panting in a trough of dead air, heat, and high humidity. Ellie took the turtle out of the trunk. It was still struggling, although it must have been weakened by asphyxiation and heat. She took a large knife, like a cleaver, and with one swipe cut off the turtle's head. Then she detached the carapace and said, "Look! Eggs." There were strings of unlaid eggs inside the exposed body. "This will make good soup." The whole thing was chopped into pieces and plopped into boiling water for the soup. It was good. I did not dwell upon the butchering techniques.

After the soup had been started, Ellie asked me a question I could not understand. Ten-year-old Liza tried to help. "She wants a thing but I can't say it right. Do you have one?" It sounded to me like "bimble jug." My bewilderment cleared in a moment when I saw what Ellie was trying to do. She had two flat tires on her car, and two new tires to put on as replacements, but she had no way of raising the car. She was asking for a bumper jack, which I did have. Together, she and I changed the tires. The replacements she put on were not really new, one being a retread, and the other a used tire, but they were better than any the car sported at the time. Many of the Indians are too poor to buy new tires, so they must make do with retreads and second hands. They often drive on tires which are absolutely slick, and they rarely carry spares. Ellie's car had been sitting useless for some weeks because of the flats. My rent payment to her had enabled her to buy the tires, and she was very pleased to have the car in running condition again, although it was a matter of only a short time before something else went wrong.

Although several men with steady jobs buy new cars, the cars owned by most of the Indians are not in very good condition. They are bought second or third hand, and often have serious mechanical problems. However, a number of the men have picked up a surprising knowledge of auto mechanics—surprising because not only are they illiterate but some of the most skilled men cannot even speak any English. I watched one of the self-taught mechanics take an engine from a 1958 Ford and put it into another old car which had a better body. The resultant hybrid ran. The owner spoke no English at all, yet he was sought out for car work by almost everyone who had car trouble. When new parts were needed, he sometimes sent an English-speaking man into town with a description of what he wanted. A far commoner way of making repairs, however, was to take various items from broken cars and combine them to make one vehicle which ran. The "mechanic" loved to work on cars and told me that his greatest wish was that he could own a garage and make a living in auto mechanics.

In general the people are very dextrous with their hands, and either out of natural inclination, or need, have learned to do much of their own repair work. Most of the ten CBS homes had electric washing machines which broke down from time to time. Repairmen would not come out to the reservation even if the Indians were able to pay for their services, but one of the Indian men taught himself enough about the workings of the washers so that he was able to repair any breakdown which occurred during the years I was there. The electrical wiring in the houses was done properly by the electricians when the houses were built, but much of the wiring in the chickees was potentially dangerous—overloads on the lines, and worn, exposed wires, most of which were too close to the water that was always underfoot during the wet season. Yet I never heard of electrical fires or of anyone getting severe shocks.

Some of the chickees still are not wired for electricity. Consequently those families have no refrigeration or electrical appliances. They still cook over open fires and use kerosene lamps. But more and more people are having their camps electrified. I frequently visited one camp where there was no electricity. It was the camp of an old woman who lived alone. The site was somewhat isolated and in a dense thicket of palmetto and brush, approached by a narrow path through overgrown vegetation. It consisted of three chickees (living, cooking, and storage) that were well surrounded by tropical foliage, and always kept very tidy. The old lady made hides into buckskin, the only person who still did so, and I spent many hours watching her work. The hunters sold or gave her the hides from the deer they killed, and she scraped and manipulated, and smoked the hides into pliable leather. Some of the skins were sold to people who wanted them as collector's items. I bought several. But others she sold to Indians who used them for items they made for the Arts and Crafts store. Another old lady, living with her daughter and grandchildren, still made the old-time flat baskets. She was the only person who could complete the rims, although some of the other women knew how to weave the bottom and sides. The baskets are either flat rounded squares with a closely woven bottom, or made with open weave bottoms for sifting. No one uses baskets any longer, and the baskets which the old woman made were all sold to tourists or other outsiders who wanted them for curios or collections. The material used is palmetto fibers, and the baskets while attractive are not examples of a high level of basket art. The Seminole never made baskets of the high degree of excellence of those made by some other southeastern Indians, the Chitimacha, for example.

## Big Cypress and American Society

One of the first things an outsider notices about the Big Cypress people is their shyness. They are perceptibly shyer than the Creek at Brighton or the other Mikasuki at Hollywood. They are, of course, much more isolated. Indeed, it is hard to get to know Big Cypress people because they are so reluctant to talk to strangers, and most of them speak no English. Even those who do will not speak much or often pretend that they cannot speak English until they have become accustomed to the stranger. They are not only shy; they are suspicious too, for they have not always been treated well by outsiders. They have been tricked and cheated more than once, and they always fear it may happen again.

Their feeling toward outside society is ambivalent however, for the outside offers them their only entertainment and escape from the endless boredom of the reservation. Boredom is a great problem there. It has more socially disruptive effects among the men than among the women. The women, even those who have been to school, still find their lives occupied by the family. Household responsibilities have remained much the same for them. Once they are married, the babies come along with only a few years between, and during their twenties, thirties, and forties, the women follow the age-old patterns of maternal behavior. The older women spend much of their increasing leisure making crafts for sale or clothes for their families. Women's time is productively occupied.

It is the men, particularly the young men, who are disorganized and listless. Labor is seasonal, and in the off-season there is nothing to do. Even work on their cattle does not take up much of their time. The men may have had some education, but whether or not there has been formal schooling, they have had more experience with the outside world than have most of the women, and this experience often leaves them frustrated and in many cases discontent. They feel neglected, frustrated, and bored. A few have turned to alcohol, at least upon occasion. More of a problem are those who have started gas sniffing, a practice which involves soaking rags in gasoline and sniffing the fumes until euphoria is achieved. Two men have actually become genuine addicts, showing withdrawal symptoms when they cannot get gas. The practice is to sniff gas until hunger drives them to find food. Afterwards they may break into the school or a house or steal money and then the state police are called in. Because of the unwillingness to interfere with other people, even with their own children, Indians do not try very hard to stop those who sniff gas. The doctor has tried to explain the dangers of addiction, but he has not been successful in stopping the spread of this practice. Gas sniffing does not fall under state jurisdiction like narcotics addiction, and unless a crime is committed while under the influence, there is no sanction applied.

Though the outsider may consider the Indians very shy in white-Indian contacts, the Indians are quiet people even within their own culture. When they speak, they gaze at the ground or the far horizon, or any place other than at the person they speak to. This is proper etiquette for Indians, not mere shyness. Their voices are hushed. Few arguments result in shouting or even loud voices. Angry Indians usually separate rather than quarrel. But with all their quietness, they have an easy and surprisingly sophisticated sense of humor, even with strangers. Once when I was making a survey of electrical appliances, I asked a woman whether she owned a vacuum cleaner. She turned and indicated her seven-year-old son who was eating everything in sight, and said, "There's my vacuum cleaner." The humor comes as a delightful surprise to the outsider who often considers Indians cold and withdrawn. They like to laugh. Off the reservation their behavior patterns are a means of protection against the uncertainty of white behavior and the Indian's insecurity in a world not his own. The children in the Clewiston schools have the reputation of being shy almost to the point of paranoia. Sometimes this shyness extends into the high school years and beyond. Often, however, it is not much more than traditional respect patterns or a buffer in facing an uncertain world.

The Indians are a racial minority in an area with a history of racial intolerance. Restaurants have often refused admission to Indians or ignored them until the Indians were embarrassed and finally departed. In many public places the Indians feel oppressed and discriminated against. The treatment of the Indians by town merchants has been typical of patterns of prejudice in the South. Indians are allowed to shop for groceries, but are often made to feel unwelcome in many eating establishments and soda fountains. At drive-ins they can expect to be

*A meal—dress of the 1920s.*

*Costumes of the 1920s.*

waited on, but not at the better restaurants. The stores selling cheap clothing cater to the Indians, poor white, and blacks. The more "exclusive" fashionable stores may snub such customers, or at least the Indians fear that they will be snubbed.

The preference for traditional clothes is still strong among the women in their middle years and older, and they still wear their hair long in traditional styles. A few of the very old women continue to brush their hair up and over a frame which forms a brim or sunshade over the forehead. Women of middle years have long hair which they usually braid or make into a bun on the top of the head or at the nape of the neck. The younger women have succumbed to permanents and the latest styles in coiffeur and dresses. The daughter of one of the leaders has her hair done in Clewiston occasionally, but she is an exception. Other young women give each other home permanents.

Few females wear shorts or slacks. Only a few younger women and school children were observed in sports garments of this nature. The older people consider the clothing worn by white women to be immodest, skirts too short, and dresses too tight, but they do not directly chastise the girls for wearing them. Rather, their disapproval comes out in the form of gossip, which is quite effective on all but the very young.

Adult women wear long skirts, ankle length, with one or more strips of traditional designs sewn around them. All women and older girls know how to make these colorful strips, which come in many different designs and colors. A really fancy skirt may have as many as seven rows of designs. Each color in the strip is a separate piece of cloth. The best comparison to this type of strip sewing is patchwork, but even the finest patchwork is gross compared to the delicate intricacy of the strip design. Although some of the designs have been popular for years, new ones are invented all the time. An inventor considers it flattering if other women copy her design.

A cape tops off the banded skirt; heavy cotton in winter, sheer material in summer or for dress up. A blouse is worn under the cape. Not many women wear beads, which in earlier times were piled high around the neck in 50 or more strands until it appeared that the neck was stretched. Sometimes the quantity of beads worn would weigh as much as 25 pounds! Although one old lady put on several pounds of beads when I took her picture, none of the younger women ever wore them in my presence.

The men wear jeans, shirts, broad-brimmed hats, and boots when they ride horseback. The young men dress much like their counterparts in the general population. Tennis shoes, loafers, and sandals are worn, but there are still many people of all ages and both sexes who go barefoot in spite of the teaching about hookworm. On festive occasions the costumes become very gay and gaudy. Men dress up in shirts made of bands of the colorful strips, and the women wear their most elaborate skirts and capes. At the Powwow and Field Day festivities contests for the most colorful and well made traditional clothing are held. There is also a contest for the best application of the strip designs to new fashions. In town the clothing, hair fashions, and darker skins are highly visible. The Indians, especially the older ones, are set apart from the general population by their appearance.

*A woman displaying a skirt she has just made for the author.*

With the advent of electric power, television became popular at Big Cypress. It is now a major form of amusement and information about the rest of the world. The battery operated radio, however, remains the most commonly owned source of entertainment. The music from radios in camps where teenagers live is continuous and syncopated. The young folks have the same attraction to rock and roll as the same age group in the general population, several have phonographs. The noise level seems all out of proportion to the usual quiet domesticity, but no one ever suggests that the children turn down the sound. Even the older people seem to enjoy the popular music. Radio and television, with the ubiquitous comic book, are the only entertainment for the Indians on the reservation. There was once a recreation hall which was used for sewing classes, meetings, and other more serious activities, as well as for recreation, but it was turned into a short-lived woodwork shop. Since the building contained much valuable machinery, even though it was no longer being used, it was locked up, and now there is no recreation hall and no access to the woodwork equipment either. Not only is the reservation far from the town, and there is no public transportation, but many people are too poor or too shy to go to town just for fun anyhow.

Needless to say, television, radio, and comics give the Indians a rather unrealistic, not to say warped view of outside society. Very few people can read, and no one gets newspapers or magazines regularly. The outside world is seen by many naive Indians as full of secret agents and Hollywood characters. One older Indian man at first refused to talk to me because he thought I was "part of the

FBI or a communist or something like that." Even the magazines available at the clinic do not give the Indians a different slant on life off the reservation, for all the women do is look at pictures since they cannot read. That is, of course, the advantage of the comic book, for it is made to be looked at rather than read, and young and old thumb these publications until they are virtually in shreds.

The young Indians are eager for trips to town. When anyone goes, he can be sure of a car full of passengers. The ride itself is dull, over prairie and swamp for nearly an hour, but it is a break in the monotony. There is a library in Clewiston, but only one Indian claimed to patronize it. The other people go to the movies, bars, or just wander around. Some summers there is a girls' softball league on which some of the teenage girls from Big Cypress play. They enjoy softball very much, but the trip to and from Clewiston amounts to nearly 100 miles, and transportation often becomes a problem. For their part, the people of Clewiston do not try very hard to get the Big Cypress people to join in public events, although the school sponsored athletic programs are open to all the students.

When asked what the boys do for fun at Big Cypress, one teenage respondent replied,

> We play softball or basketball. Most people here just walk up and down the road, or stay home and play cards maybe, or just sit. Maybe hunt or fish. I like to fish. My whole family goes. Sometimes we sit out in the chickee at school, and talk to each other, but we don't go to each other's house.

He went on to say,

> In town you have more things to do, like go to movies and so on, but down here on Saturday, they just go up and down the road, maybe drink beer if they have money. Just walk and sit around at the school. I wish we had the recreation building back again. There are places like youth centers in town I've heard.
>
> No, I have never been to a youth center, but seems like they would be a good thing.

Before Alligator Alley was built few people went to Hollywood on the coast during the week. The trip was long and expensive, and the Indians' cars were apt to break down all too often. Now trips to the coast are more frequent. Some Indians go to tourist centers on the east or west coasts to make a little money during the season. These trips rarely mean contact with white Floridians as neighbors and friends, but usually as employers or customers for Indian crafts.

The means of transportation is always a privately owned car because there is no public transportation of any sort. One may catch a bus in Clewiston bound for the east or west coastal towns, but a car is necessary to get to Clewiston. The state of Florida does not charge Indians for their license plates, which are distinguished from the plates of the general public by the words: "Seminole Indian." The cars, usually used, are purchased on credit in Immokalee, Clewiston, or in one of the coastal cities. Many people at Big Cypress believe that the used-car dealers cheat the Indians, who do not know enough about financing or auto mechanics to purchase wisely. The prevailing belief among used-car dealers is that Indians are poor financial risks whose cars will probably have to be repossessed with considerable trouble. Both groups are right in part. There are some Indians who do not keep up payments and who treat the cars so badly that they are ruined, and there are some dealers who deliberately sell the Indians bad cars. However, there are also those merchants who go out of their way to help the Indians, and there are Big Cypress people who have excellent credit ratings among the Clewiston tradesman.

There is very little group cohesiveness at Big Cypress. Traditionally the people lived in isolated camps in the Big Cypress Swamp or the Everglades proper, and while there was some visiting between these camps, decisions were never made that would be binding on more than one residential unit, for there was no one who could make a decision binding on several camp groups. Communication was slow and uncertain. When the various camps were in agreement and acted in concert, it was usually because the adaptive requirements were such as to produce mutually similar responses to similar needs and situations. Households are cohesive units, but interaction among members of different camps, except for the adolescents, is between relatives more than between neighbors. There are households of single old people who are cared for and visited by relatives. They prefer to live a solitary existence in their own chickees rather than joining other aged people in a single camp. They shun dependence in old age and consider maintaining their camps by themselves preferable to moving into a chickee within a younger relative's camp. The agency feels concerned about these solitary individuals, but the old people themselves prefer to be alone.

The people who are now the adults at Big Cypress grew up in a tradition of autonomy for each camp. There never had been intercamp planning except for the Green Corn Dance arrangements, and this ceremony has not been performed at Big Cypress within this decade. Other communal occasions are very rare, if not nonexistent. No one can remember joint activities of any importance among the various camps. People still do not think in terms of common goals, although there has been a greater tendency on the part of some individuals in this direction since tribal reorganization. The initiation of an all-tribe annual powwow did result in some organized planning although many Indians have never participated. While much of the organizational effort has been provided by the agency, little by little more Indians are becoming involved.

In 1962, at Hollywood Reservation, the Seminole Tribe held its first powwow. It was intended solely for the Indians, although some non-Indians were invited to attend. At first the powwow only received some minor publicity in the local newspapers. Indians from all three reservations took part, and the following year the second annual powwow was held at Brighton, and the third in 1964 at Big Cypress. The following two years, Hollywood and Brighton each hosted the affair again. Up to this point it had remained entertainment for the Indians only, a day for them to spend together. There were athletic events, an arts and crafts show and competition, a "Miss Seminole" contest, a baby contest, a judging of the finest traditional and modern applications of the sewn strips, and a big meal for all.

When the powwow was held at Big Cypress, the women of the reservation worked until late the previous night preparing all the food. Ellie, in whose household I was living at the time, helped cut up and cook a slaughtered steer. In addition to the meat there were salads, fry bread, sofki, iced tea, swamp cabbage, rice, baked beans, and cookies. There was food for about 300, and what was left over the cooks divided up to eat the next day. Although there were few non-Indians in attendance, those who were there ran the powwow. Agency officials judged the contests, ran the arts and crafts show and athletic competition, and supervised the sanitation. It was not like the powwows of the western Indians. There was no drumming, singing or dancing.

Little by little publicity about the powwow spread. More and more tourists began attending. It became obvious that the powwow could become profitable if held in an easily accessible location with wider publicity. Hollywood Reservation on U.S. Highway 441 was the ideal spot. Tourists coming to see the powwow would spend money in the Arts and Crafts shop and snack bar. They would pay for a tour through the reconstructed traditional Seminole village. For a price, they could also watch alligator wrestling. Alligator wrestling was never a traditional sport, but rather quite a recent development to attract tourists. Very few Big Cypress men ever engaged in this activity, almost all wrestlers coming from Hollywood. It is very dangerous, but it does offer an income for only a few hours work. All these factors—the shop, the traditional village, the snack bar, and the alligator wrestling—made a financial success of the powwow in a way that could never be duplicated at the other reservations. Dancing was added and in 1968 the event was extended to three days.

Not everyone was pleased with the change from an Indian festival to a money-making enterprise. There were enough people who wanted to continue the nonprofit sort of entertainment that had been offered by the earlier powwows. Therefore a Field Day was instituted at the other reservations, held each year for the Indians themselves and specially invited guests. The Field Day is not intended to be a financial success.

There are certain problems that all camps have had to face in the new political situation in which they agreed to become subject to the state laws of Florida. These problems include community sanitation, garbage disposal, latrine construction, drunken driving, etc. Few people have demonstrated any sense of civic responsibility in trying to solve these problems. They have been seen as individual problems, not as public affairs. For example, when the tribe had sufficient funds, the directors hired a garbage collector to make regular pickups at the camps. He collected the trash and took it off to a dump which had been excavated for this specific purpose. When the tribal funds ran too low to support this service, the job was abolished, and the officers held public meetings in an attempt to find a community solution to the problem of sanitary disposal of wastes. There were disappointingly few people turning out for these meetings, and the people who did attend were the responsible citizens who were not creating the problem. They could not find a solution which would be accepted by the other members of society. Consequently, it was left to the inhabitants of each camp to get their garbage to the dump by themselves. No committee formed to consider community action. No organizational attempt was made to divide up the work according to some sort of schedule. No individual or group recommendations were made. The Indians who had been taking proper care of their own trash continued to do so. Those who had refused to be responsible for their trash also refused to go to the meetings. But even the seemingly more civic-minded group could not come up with any ideas about community action on the issue.

The result was that there were camps where trash was disposed of by throwing it in the canals and irrigation ditches, or by piling it up on the periphery of the camp area. No social pressure was brought to bear on these miscreants, and even the county sanitation could not enforce sanitary practices in absence of community support. No one ever volunteered his services as surrogate or collector for the reservation. Individual households functioned in this matter as they wished, regardless of whether the neighboring households were being endangered by their lack of proper sanitation. Eventually the problem was solved when the tribe found money to hire another garbage collector.

The same situation existed in the matter of latrine construction in the days before the self-help housing project. The county health officials explained many times that the erection and use of properly constructed latrines would help eliminate the hookworm hazard and dysentery which is an epidemic at Big Cypress, but there was no community action or any sanctions that would have made the residents observe sanitary procedures in this matter either, even though all the children of the reservation have been endangered by the unsanitary conditions.

Lack of community responsibility and cohesiveness is noticeable also in the control of adolescents. While these young people have not caused great social disruptions, there are some indications that all is not well. Some of the boys have taken to weekend drinking bouts, but more serious is the practice of gas sniffing

*Field Day (Powwow) at Big Cypress—contest for most elaborate dress in traditional style.*

which can become an addiction. The public health doctor has tried to explain to the parents that this is a potentially dangerous practice, but the parents merely shrug it off and say that they have no way of preventing the boys from doing whatever they want. One father of a teenage boy said that he would thrash his son if he ever caught him sniffing gas. He was the only person to take a firm stand on the issue. Others questioned said they had no intention of interfering, even though their own sons might be involved. They felt it was wrong to try to regulate behavior by concerted action.

The teenagers are frustrated by the comparison between their life and what they have seen of life off the reservation. They cannot participate in wider American society, and they react to their frustrations by gas sniffing, drinking, apathy, and general discontent.

"It isn't any of my business." "That's their affair, not mine." "I don't want to tell them what to do, and I don't want them to tell me what to do." Comments such as these express general reticence about entering into controversies, problem situations, or intruding in any way upon another's privacy. If a request for help or information is made, most Indians are glad to respond, but they never enter into affairs of another household unbidden, even to help. Joint action toward solution to problems of adolescent boredom and resultant misbehavior does not occur. The only social affairs ever arranged for the young (or for the old, for that matter) while I was there were the work of outsiders, the agency, the extension service, or the teachers. The Big Cypress residents did not plan for any community social activities.

The Big Cypress inhabitant talks in terms of "I" instead of "we." It is rare that a person refers to the community as a group. Individual solutions to individual problems are sought regardless of how many others may have had identical problems. Even community efforts such as the cattle program are largely viewed individualistically, from the standpoint of what is best for "my" herd, not what must be the program for development of the total cattle industry. No one ever suggests organizing for the purpose of gathering and disseminating information or making recommendations.

The Big Cypress residents think of themselves first of all as Mikasuki. They do not usually refer to themselves as Big Cypress people or as Seminole. When they wish to discriminate between themselves and Brighton residents, they use the categories "Mikasuki" and "Creek." However, in considering the incorporated tribe as opposed to white society, they may say "Seminole," although "Indian" or "Red People" are also terms frequently employed. Big Cypress people identify with the Creek only when they join forces to resist some sort of pressure from the outside. Under normal conditions they rather carefully maintain a separate identity. Creek living at Big Cypress as a result of marriage or because they are working there are never part of the in-group, even those spouses who have lived at Big Cypress for years. In referring to them, someone is certain to remark that they are Creek, or that they really belong to the Brighton group. Children of Mikasuki women who married Creek and went to Brighton to live are welcomed at Big Cypress as proper Mikasuki because their mothers were Mikasuki. In general, the existence of the two separate groups is conspicuous not only because the two languages are mutually unintelligible, but because the two communities foster this division by training the young to continue it. Each group considers its own members slightly superior.

As far as I could ascertain, the Big Cypress people either as a single community or jointly with the Creek do not consider themselves part of any larger group in the general society. They realize that they are American citizens, and some of the young men have served or are presently serving in the armed forces, but they give no indication of viewing themselves as part of a larger society, that is, Floridians or southerners. They feel themselves definitely set apart from any other ethnic group within Florida—Negro, Puerto Rican, Mexican —although most of the Indian mixed marriages which occur are between the latter two groups and Indian women. Some racial prejudice learned from the southern white population's attitude toward Negroes has begun to seep into Big Cypress even though there was Negro intermarriage with the Indians in the recent past. The Indians show no desire to belong to any of these larger social groupings, and even when married to a member of another group continue to consider their own group the Big Cypress community.

Indians are in general not only mistrustful of outsiders, but often feel nothing in common with them. The interests of the two groups are completely different. Although television has brought intimate glimpses into the family, social, and business affairs of the outside world, the Indians see no correspondence to their own lives. The world of the whites remains totally separate from the Indian's world. Very few Indians have ever been in a white man's home, and most of their contact is through merchants, the agency, television, radio, and the omnipresent comic book, all of which present rather unrealistic elements of out-side life. There are few genuine friendships between a white person and an Indian outside of the Indian and Mexican or Puerto Rican marriages. Even though the Indian may desire the appliances and material goods of the outer society, he feels no particular pride in the "American way of life" or in democratic insti-tutions. Indeed, he is largely unaware of them. The giant economic enterprises— mass production, international reputation, and urban culture—are unknown to the Indian. His horizons do not extend beyond the prairie and swamp. To him Big Cypress is the best place in the world, and only one person interviewed wanted to live anywhere else. What the residents want from the outside is modern conveniences and a market for their cattle and crafts. Big Cypress is home; it is cherished.

# 4

# Health, Education, and Religion

## Health

A VERY IMPORTANT CONTACT with white society is the public health nurse, a woman liked, trusted, and respected. The clinic is always full of mothers with children, teenagers, and a sprinkling of old folks. They come not only for treatment, but for social reasons. The two mornings the clinic is open offer mild excitement for these people.

Mikasuki mothers are prompt to get their children to the clinic for treatment and for the preventive shots. The nurse sends the message that it is time for a booster, and the mothers appear with children in tow. However, just to be certain that they are not overlooking any possible benefits, many Indians still go to the medicine man in addition to the public health clinic. It is genuinely believed that modern scientific medicine is very effective, and there is no better proof of this belief than the fact that all the medicine men go to the nurse for treatment themselves. But at the same time modern medicine does not cure all ailments. The medicine men offer therapy for bad dreams and unrequited love as well as treatment for disease and injury. These men are quite adept in setting bones for a simple fracture, they know how to stop severe bleeding, and the most famous medicine man has a tremendous knowledge of herbs (Sturtevant 1954: *passim*)

There are three practicing medicine men of importance, and one or two others are believed to have specialized skill and knowledge. It troubles the Indians to know that instead of payment in the traditional cloth or live animals, some of the medicine men are now asking for money. Occasionally a medicine man comes in from Oklahoma and stays for three or four weeks doing cures. These western medicine men are said to charge as much as twenty dollars per cure.

The new clinic is a modern air-conditioned building joined by a breezeway to the new school, also air-conditioned. The old clinic, which was in use during the early years of my fieldwork, was an old frame structure raised off the ground on cement blocks. The clinic proper was half of the building. The other half, consisting of two bedrooms, a kitchen, a living-room/dining room, bathroom and screened porch, was the living quarters for the summer school teacher or for government guests at other times. The whole edifice became the headquarters for the nursery instituted under the Community Action Program in 1966.

During the time I was at Big Cypress before the new clinic was built, the public health nurse visited Big Cypress two mornings a week. On the appointed days people would often begin to gather at the clinic before the nurse arrived, for they came not only for her services and advice, but often to break the monotony and join with friends for a few moments of talk in the front porch of the clinic, which had glass louvered windows and a room air-conditioner. It made a cool meeting place in the summer. In the winter, except for the really cold days, the windows were opened to the breezes. The old clinic was very close to the community mail station. In those days mail came to Big Cypress three times a week and people picked up their mail and visited the clinic at the same time. Now mail is delivered to individual mail boxes which stand along the road.

It was always interesting to go to the clinic. In one small space I could see and talk with many people, and there were things I learned about the Seminole at the clinic which I could not have found out elsewhere. They were very fond of the nurse, and they sometimes told her about their problems other than those pertaining to their health, but above all it was there that I could observe the reactions to the preventive shots, curative pills, and general health problems.

Old Lucille, a medicine woman who had specialized in female ills, childbirth, sterility, and sick children, was a regular visitor at the clinic. She told me that she could cure sprains, stomach upset, diarrhea, periodic pain and earaches, and could deliver babies. She doctored with herbs and songs. Lucille was one of the oldest inhabitants of Big Cypress. Her actual birthdate was uncertain, but it was thought to be about 1880. One time when she dressed up for me to take her picture, she put on the pounds of beads once favored by all the Seminole women, and also a sort of coin or medal pinned to her cape with a safety pin. She said it had been her mother's, and it represented the time of trouble, by which she meant the third Seminole War, 1856. The old lady came often to the clinic for a B-12 shot. Many of the older people got B-12 shots regularly for anemia resulting from hookworm infestation. Old Lucille had a hemoglobin count that stood at 4.5, whereas the normal count is 12 to 15. A count below 10 is considered anemic. Lucille's count was no lower than that of a number of other old people, and it did not seem to affect her vitality. The nurse recounted to me that Lucille had taken her one day to find some swamp apples and that the nurse, whose hemoglobin count was normal and who was a young woman, was tired out sooner than the old woman by that hike through the swamp. A story which I heard several times concerned another elderly woman whose recurring hookworm infestation puzzled the public health authorities, who told her to wear tennis shoes to prevent re-infestation. But still one cure followed another, and the old lady became re-infested. The puzzle was cleared up one day when the nurse discovered that the old Indian wore her tennis shoes only to the clinic because she liked to please the nurse. She had never really understood what the shoes were supposed to do, and so finding them uncomfortable, she removed them once out of sight of the clinic. The hookworm problem was not confined to the old. One young girl had been so badly infested that she required hospitalization.

Hookworms are bloodsucking intestinal parasites, one species of which is found in man, another in cats and dogs. The worms attach themselves to the wall of the small intestine and suck blood. The female lays thousands of eggs which are passed out of the host in the feces, and these eggs hatch into larvae under favorable conditions of warmth and moisture. Such are the conditions of Big Cypress swamp. The larvae live near the surface of the soil, and whenever suitable hosts appear (bare-footed in the case of humans), they burrow into their skins. There is some reason to believe that in an area of heavy infestation by larvae it is possible to pick them up from the tall grasses, and therefore sandals may not offer adequate protection, so the health officials try to get everyone to wear tennis shoes, which cover the tops of the feet as well as the soles. Since at the time of this fieldwork very few of the Big Cypress people had toilets or sanitary privies, there were many areas where it was possible to pick up the infestation.

After penetrating the skin of the host, the larvae find their way to the blood stream and from there to the lungs, where they produce irritation and coughing on the part of the host. They may then be coughed up in the mucous and swallowed, passing through the stomach to the intestines where the whole cycle repeats itself. They result is severe anemia if not treated. Rural populations of the southeastern United States have suffered heavy infestation by hookworm in the past, but the incidence is much lower today because of excellent therapy and the increase in sanitation. The Big Cypress Indians are regularly encouraged to have fecal examinations. The children and the old are the two age groups which today show the highest incidence.

Dog and cat worms produce a peculiar pathology among humans. Indian children playing on the ground in dirt contaminated by dog and cat feces develop skin disorders from the hookworm species infesting the animals. Those larvae do not enter the children's circulatory system but rather burrow under the children's skin producing winding tunnels which are called "creeping eruption." The children scratch the itching eruptions often furthering the discomfort by infecting the skin with dirt. It is a difficult disorder to cure and a nasty disease to see, scabby skin crusted with blood and dirt, the worm burrows showing clearly their tortuous routes under the skin.

Twice a month a doctor under contract to the Bureau of Indian Affairs goes to the reservation. He treats the more serious medical problems and does obstetrical examinations of the pregnant women. The Indians also go to one of two contract doctors at Clewiston or to the hospital there for emergency treatment or for the delivery of babies, or for any other disability requiring special treatment or equipment. Occasionally an individual is sent to the hospital in Ft. Lauderdale. Otherwise, the nurse takes care of all therapy. Dysentery is endemic, and a little more than three per cent of the population at Big Cypress is diabetic. The nurse gives insulin shots to most of the diabetics, although she taught the daughters of one woman to give their mother injections.

Any clinic day produces a cross section of the Big Cypress population coming in for treatment of some sort. Parents are very conscientious about bringing their children for their immunization shots and boosters. The nurse keeps records indicating when the next shot is due, and when she sends out the word, the Indians appear promptly. A reminder is enough. The adults also get a series of booster shots, especially tetanus shots, and the men seem to enjoy making exaggerated grimaces and loud complaints to amuse the children awaiting their turn. The men stop off long enough to get their immunizations during lunch hours or on the way to work if they are employed.

Some of the children are remarkably quiet, passive almost, about their injections. Others scream as lustily as any children in the general population. The nurse keeps a supply of balloons on hand for the children. The favorite color is red, and many a child walks out of the clinic clutching a balloon while tears still stream down his cheeks.

Almost any clinic day there are mothers with badly cut children coming in for care. Broken glass, tin cans, and sharp implements lying around the camps always present obstacles. The resultant wounds are often deep and jagged. Cleaning and bandaging are inevitably followed by a tetanus shot, a red balloon, and often tears. One day while I was observing at the clinic, a young girl came in with an unusually deep and dirty gash on her foot. She had stepped on a broken "pop" bottle. The nurse treated the child, who was not one of the quiet patients. She screamed mightily as the nurse was cleaning out the gash, and she bellowed lustily at the sight of the hypodermic syringe for the tetanus shot. She left with her foot carefully bandaged in clean gauze and with instructions to put her shoes on. Two hours later I saw her on the school playground, the bandage trailing in the dirt, the foot unshod, and rapidly becoming filthy again. But her tears were gone.

As mentioned, even the old men who are the traditional "medicine men" or curers go to the clinic. It is generally believed by other Indians, and by the nurse herself, that the old curers continue to practice their own techniques while attending the clinic to make use of modern medical knowledge. No one finds this contradictory. One Big Cypress mother explained to me that there are certain disturbances for which the nurse has no cures, but which the medicine man could cure very well. Bad dreams represent one of the symptoms which medicine men have much greater curative ability than the nurse. If a child should have bad dreams, or the mother should dream her child was in danger, the proper treatment would be to go to one of the traditional curers for treatment involving songs and, frequently, some brew from herbs.

An unusual medical problem at Big Cypress is the practice of sniffing gasoline. A number of young men doubtless have tried it, but there are a few who have become genuine addicts, addicted to the point where they display definite mental deterioration in the form of a greatly shortened attention span accompanied by shakes and tremors of withdrawal symptoms when they are unable to get to a source of gasoline, such as when they are in jail, as they often are.

The technique of gas sniffing involves dipping rags in gasoline, usually by stuffing the rag into the tank of someone's car, which sometimes results in clogging the gas lines of the car when fragments of the rags remain in the tanks. With the rag soaked in gas, the sniffer breathes the fumes. Enough of this will produce cellular deterioration of the brain—irreversible deterioration, according to health authorities, and the individual's mental competence is lowered. The origin of the practice can be traced to the period following World War II when the first automobiles came to Big Cypress and gasoline was available in the tanks. No one is sure where the idea came from. The isolation of Big Cypress apparently oppressed the young men in the post-war period, and a search for release from boredom was the primary motivation behind the gas sniffing. Two fellows in that early period became addicts, but the practice was limited to them. They are now in their thirties, unfit for employment or any sort of responsibility. For a time, a number of teenagers, including some girls, and fellows in their twenties were experimenting with gas sniffing. It is said that they found relief from boredom in the practice. When gasoline storage tanks were installed at Big Cypress to supply fuel for road building machinery and government vehicles, the government soon found it necessary to enclose the installation with a cyclone fence to keep the gas from being used by the sniffers. Until the fence was erected, locks were broken and pumps were damaged by gas sniffers trying to get at the supply. A more common form of escapism, drunkenness, has not been as much of a problem in Big Cypress as on some other reservations, although it is thought by many of the Indians that the incidence of drunkenness increases sharply when income goes up. This contention appears to be supported by the increase in drinking among teenagers employed in the Neighborhood Youth Corp. They say there is nothing but beer to spend money on, and nothing else to do but drink. Beer is the common alcoholic beverage, although hard liquor is consumed whenever available. The heavy drinkers are all older men.

When I was at the clinic one morning, one of the long-time gasoline sniffers came in. He had bad sores in and around his mouth, and he was seized from time to time with uncontrollable shakes. He tried to explain to the nurse what he wanted, but she could not understand him. An Indian woman, with some high school education, who helped the nurse with the records and did necessary interpreting finally determined that he had come for a booster shot. He was a sad and unpleasant sight, small in stature and emaciated, trembling, with a very dazed look, not fearful, just totally unaware. The doctor told me that the fellow will never be normal again. He has often been picked up by police off the reservation for petty misdemeanors and put in jail, where he suffers withdrawal symptons because of his addiction to gas fumes.

Another patient was a baby whose mother said he had a fever. It was 104. The nurse instructed the mother what to do, gave the baby a shot and some aspirin, and sent them home. Then an old woman was led in by her granddaughter. She was given vitamin pills and went away helped by the grandchild. The old woman was blind and had extensive abdominal cancer on which it was useless to operate because of her age and the extent of the malignancy. She suffered very little pain however.

Next three little boys in one family were treated for skin sores. They had nasty, open, weeping wounds at which they scratched and picked, but they were in very good spirits, laughing and talking to everyone. The nurse gave the mother some medicated soap and some lotions and told her to keep the children clean and to cover the sores with the lotion. Keeping the children clean in that heat under their living conditions is a difficult task.

Two more children in another family were given medicine for diarrhea. One of the young Indian women came in to get more birth control pills. Four women at that time (1965) were taking birth control pills, and two women had had their fallopian tubes tied and cut. They each had seven children by the time they were in their mid-twenties, and drastic measures were necessary because their health had become precarious. The other women were doing well on birth control pills and were spacing their children with an eye to their ability to raise them properly and with consideration of their own health.

That year there was an epidemic of conjunctivitis at Big Cypress. It took two months to get that epidemic under control. At the same time the reservation was suffering from infectious hepatitis of almost epidemic proportions. These types of diseases are very difficult for the public health people to keep under control because of the heat and humidity and generally unsanitary conditions under which the children play. The children do not want to be isolated or to remain in bed. Some adults do not observe elementary precautions that would control the spread of contageous disease—precautions such as isolation, washing hands, not using common eating and drinking utensils, and in the case of hookworm, wearing shoes. However, most of the adults at Big Cypress bathe or shower frequently. Most camps have a well; some have water pumps and rigged up showers. Children frequent the swimming holes on the reservation in the hot weather. For those who do not have baths or showers at home, there is a building containing showers and toilets near the old school. The water is not heated, but in that climate hot water is not so important. While it is certainly true that there are some dirty Seminole Indians at any given time, I was constantly impressed with the frequency of bathing and shampooing. In addition, the Indians dislike the odor of sweat or any body odor, and deodorants were often the topic of conversation. I remember one young Indian fellow, in his mid-teens, who asked me questions about my spray deodorant which he noticed when visiting me one time. "I've never seen that kind before. Do you like it? I use Right Guard myself, but my sister likes Fresh." I used to laugh when I heard white Floridians talk about the "dirty Indians in the swamp." Many Big Cypress people come close to being fanatic about personal cleanliness. One Indian woman where I lived washed her hair, which was down to her waist, almost every day during the hot summer. I washed mine about twice a week.

The first year I lived at Big Cypress, Liza, the ten year old in the household, contracted mumps. Her neck glands were swollen and she had a high fever. But she was still responsible for two younger children in the family when the older women were away working. During the height of her fever I found her pulling the two children around in a wagon in the midday August sun! She had been with children from other camps, and, of course, the disease affected many children and not a few adults (including the two women in our household) before it ran its course by September.

Once at the clinic, after the patients had all left, the nurse, the assistant with her two children, and I had a picnic. Since there was no school that day, one of the aide's children had accompanied her mother and spent the morning at the clinic. Later in the day the older child and the father came in. The father was custodian of the clinic and school; he mowed the grass, emptied the trash, and cleaned the buildings as well as taking on any sundry tasks as required. The children had a wonderful time at lunch, thanks to the nurse, who had brought along many good things to eat: bread, cookies, coke, deviled eggs, frozen strawberries, and sandwich spreads. That was before there was a grocery store at Big Cypress, and the novelty of the food and the occasion made for high joviality. The nurse's assistant and her husband were among the better educated Indians, and their jobs were considered very desirable. For her part, the nurse found the aide invaluable because she had a great need for a trustworthy assistant and interpreter.

Big Cypress women appear unusually heavy, especially compared to the norm of feminine beauty in the outer society. I asked the doctor about the weight problem, and he told me that the health officials were worried about female obesity because it often caused complications during childbirth. Most of the diabetics are grossly overweight, and the doctor and nurse constantly urge them to diet. I observed very carefully the quantity and quality of the food eaten in the various camps where I lived and visited. The diet is varied and generally very good since the Indians eat a lot of fruits and meat with every meal. However, it is overheavy on starches and highly caloric carbonated beverages. The diabetics have been encouraged to drink artificially sweetened beverages. However well balanced the meals may be, the Indians, especially the women, simply eat too much. Many of the women who tend to start putting on weight in their teens, are from 50 to 75 pounds overweight. There are a few who weigh well over 200 pounds. Restricting food intake apparently is not understood by most of the adults, for one woman who weighed over 200 pounds told me that she had been taking diet pills for almost half a year and had not lost weight. In answer to my question, she said that she had not been eating any less because she thought all she need do was take the pills. What seems to be lacking is the motivation to diet. As one man told me, "We like big, meaty women." The combination of diet and lack of planned exercise is reinforced by a cultural preference of the men for heavy women.

Very few of the people wear glasses; two have hearing aids; and one child has braces for a crippled condition of the legs. Two old people had extensive cancer when I first went to the reservation. They have since died. One young mother is an asthmatic, a few old people have mild heart conditions, and there are two mongoloid children. Dental carries are prevalent. The medical people say it is the result of poor prophylaxis plus too much sugar in the diet from soft drinks and sweets. A number of young people have had all their upper incisors pulled. There is a dental clinic operated for two weeks in a trailer brought to the reservation just before school starts in the fall. The government pays for this service, but except in special cases does not pay for plates and bridges. For dental problems arising during the year, there are contract dentists in Clewiston to whom the Indians are sent.

However, in spite of the occasional spread of contagious disease, the frequency of skin infection, and hookworm infestation, the Big Cypress people are basically healthy. Most childhood contagious diseases have been eliminated by a program of innoculation and the vigilance of the public health nurse. There is little tuberculosis and virtually no venereal disease. The consistency with which the Indians take their children for examinations and preventative shots, the prenatal care which has resulted in mortality rates among new borns and parturient mothers no higher than among the general population, and the fact that the basic culture puts a strong emphasis on frequent showering and bathing, all result in long life expectancy and good physical conditions. The health authorities agree that compared to conditions among Indians elsewhere or among other people of equivalent income level, the Big Cypress population is in unusually fine physical condition.

Besides the nurse and doctor, there is a county sanitarian, who supervises such things as garbage disposal, public cooking, water purity, mosquito control, and vermin control. The government has sunk two wells, 90 and 125 feet deep, and put in chlorinators. Unfortunately the wells have brought in sulphur water, which though not unhealthy, is unpalatable to many. An aerator was installed on the well supplying the schools and clinic, but the last time I was in one of the CBS homes, their water was still strongly sulphurated. However, the water is pure for drinking and cooking. The CBS homes and the government buildings were alone in having a sewage disposal system in the early years of the '60s, but the new self-help housing project includes proper facilities for each camp site.

## Education

Since Florida state truancy laws apply to all Indian children, they are expected to attend school on a regular basis. There is a federal day school on the reservation going from grade one through four. In addition there are two programs for pre-schoolers, Headstart, and a day nursery, which contribute to the preparation of children for the school experience. Before the pre-school programs were developed, most children spent two years in first grade because of their lack of familiarity with English. The first year of first grade was largely devoted to teaching children essentials of English speech so that they could understand what was going on during the second year of first grade. Even now, three years after the introduction of Headstart, some children still require two years in first grade. No one at Big Cypress lives in a household in which English is spoken as the first language. In order to offer as much language as possible, for lack of language skills continues to be the major problem in education, the school is also open for eight weeks of summer when children may attend to increase academic competence and to enjoy a program of arts and crafts.

The old school is a wooden building which had all four grades in a single room under one teacher. It is now used for Headstart. The spacious new school building has all modern facilities including air-conditioning. It is large enough to divide the children into two groups, and there are now two teachers. In addition there are young Indian women hired as teaching aids, and others to cook the midday meal supplied to the students.

The school grounds are extensive, containing many pieces of playground equipment. Indoor facilities are new and very up-to-date: sinks, desks, a piano, bookcases, a movie projector, and all kinds of school supplies, including, of course, many books suitable for the ages of the students from texts to encyclopedias.

Starting with the fifth grade, the children go to school in Clewiston. The trip to and from Clewiston must be made on a school bus because there is no other means of transportation. Commuting children therefore spend two hours each day just riding the bus, which leaves for the reservation immediately after school closes. All extracurricular activities and such school facilities as the library are unavailable to the Seminole students. Immokalee is closer to Big Cypress, but it is in a different county, and Clewiston is in the proper school district. Many students and parents think it is unfortunate that the Big Cypress children cannot go to Immokalee because they believe they would get a better education there. Immokalee is a shipping center which during the winter months has a population of Mexicans, Puerto Ricans, Negroes, Whites, and some Indians. The Immokalee school system is prepared to handle cultural and linguistic variety. Clewiston, on the other hand, is quite homogeneous, a town which directs its major effort toward its college-bound students. Until the mid-sixties, the school system was segregated in Clewiston. I was told that that was the reason Indian children did not go there until recently. (The first Indians graduated from Clewiston High School in 1963). For many years the Clewiston board insisted that any Indians attending their schools would have to go to the Negro school. The Indians refused, preferring to go to Bureau of Indian Affairs boarding schools or drop out entirely.

Because they consider the Immokalee system better, some Indians send their children to live with relatives in the small Indian community there. Several children were started in the Immokalee school in first grade because living in Immokalee would force them to use English a lot more frequently than at Big Cypress, where they spoke Mikasuki to everyone except the teachers. One boy in the junior high school said,

> I know I get a better education in Immokalee. My English is better because I talk it more. I'm ahead in classwork and the books I read. The other kids in Immokalee don't look down on me either. I'd like to teach social studies. That's my favorite subject. I'd have to go to college and study. I think I could get into college if I try hard and keep my grades up. English is my hardest subject. Outside of English I get good grades—better than average.

In all fairness, it must be pointed out that many Indians going to Clewiston were very content and defended their school loyally. However, regardless of the school attended, the Indian children have an inferior command of the English language. The first girl to graduate from Clewiston high went to business college. She said,

> After I graduated from high school I went to business college because in high school I didn't take courses that would prepare me for the university. I realized that there was nothing for me to do. I had no training. All I could do would be go back to the reservation. I thought maybe I'd go to Haskell Institute, but I did not want to go so far away. I did want to go on to school and find some job and work. I thought bookkeeping would be good because I had had that in high school and loved it. So I enrolled in the business college, but my English was so bad I had an awful time. I had to take three months extra because of English courses. But that helped me. I never did understand why my English was so bad—whether it was my fault or whether it was the English I had in high school. I thought I got by in high school; they never told me that my English was so inferior, but it was not good enough for college. It was *terrible*. I had to attend special classes.

Even though the children are given an extra year in first grade, they are not up to grade level when they move on to Clewiston schools at fifth grade. There are several reasons for this retardation, the most important being the language handicap. Except in the school situation, the children do not practice English after they have learned it. However, there is more involved than language deficiency. Three other factors are particularly important: poor study habits, lack of encouragement, and little relevance or application of learning to life.

Poor study habits result from the lack of home example. Necessary solitude and quiet and a general atmosphere conducive to study are not found in many households. There are no reference books in the homes. Indeed, there are no books at all in most homes except for the omnipresent comic book. Very few children have any place where they can study without interruption or where they can keep academic materials. The general absence of outside reading and inability to take notes and review past material become really serious by the high school years. Such gaps in experience and training are not easy to make up later under the even greater pressures of advanced academic work. The parents of the children are usually illiterate and cannot help the children with any sort of school work, and school life is so far from the experience of the parents that they hesitate to give any advice or make any suggestions. Some of the children interpret the apparent lack of parental interest as a sign that the parents do not care about their children, but in almost all cases that is an erroneous conclusion. The parents simply do not have the knowledge to help, and they are not achievement oriented.

> Parents show so little affection—even if they love their children, they don't show it. Either they don't think they should or what—I don't know. But there are a whole lot of families here won't show their affection. Like I was telling you, I heard some kids say "my mother doesn't care whether I go to school or not so why should I go? My parents don't come to see whether I'm in bed at night and stuff like that." Kids like that going to school with white children can see that those kids get encouragement and affection from their mother and father, and the Indians don't. I think that is one of the biggest downfalls we have here.

Another informant who had been to Clewiston schools said,

> My father cared about us. When it was cold to go to school, he made sure we were warm and didn't leave on an empty stomach, and a lot of parents, I don't think, do that. They don't get up and see that their kids are getting ready for school and give a hand or something. When the mother has to work in the fields, she has to get up before the kids go to school. You know in the winter most of the mothers work in the fields.

Parental encouragement was a strong force in the education of the one Big Cypress resident to get a degree beyond high school.

> Another thing that was important in my childhood schooling was that my daddy always looked at my report card when I brought it home from school. Now my father didn't really know what it meant, and he couldn't read, but he always looked at my report card and made me feel that he cared how I did in school. Most other parents never did this. In fact, most of the kids never showed their parents their report cards. But my daddy made me feel that it was important to him. I told him what the marks stood for. It was a rewarding experience for me. He took the time.

However, when Indian students have finished high school, it has usually been in spite of rather than because of parents. Encouragement to continue education has come from the branch of education of the Seminole Agency or from various outsiders who have come to know individual Indian adolescents in school or in some other context. Some parents appear to have actually discouraged their children because they could not see why the children should spend the season of peak employment in school when they could be out in the fields getting paid. Many students have concurred with that view point. They cannot see any connection between schooling and employment. Therefore they drop out of school in order to take jobs, thereby limiting their future employment to field labor. They ask why they should get a high school diploma when they cannot make any more money with it than without it.

> Seems like they're (the teachers) always getting at you to do something—always on your back. What good does it do? I can work in the fields without an education.

It is true that up till now there have been few jobs requiring a high school education, but the employment picture is expected to change with the completion of the access road to the toll road. Few Indians have planned for a new employment situation by staying in school. They see only the immediate income from field labor, not future income dependent upon more education.

By 1965 there were only eight high school graduates at Big Cypress, two from Clewiston High School, the others from Indian boarding schools. Predictably there is a great difference between the way the graduates and the dropouts view education. Of the educated group, many more tend to give credit to their parents for support and encouragement. The members of this group also had some goal in mind, better employment opportunities or a desire to help their people. The dropouts spoke disparagingly of their teachers and were skeptical about benefiting from education in any way. None of the latter reported any parental interest in their schooling. However, the noninvolvement on the part of the parents is difficult to gauge and may be more apparent than real. I found that while parents may feel that they know too little to say anything, they often, when questioned, expressed very affirmative views and regret that the child had decided to leave school. Here are two statements, one by a boy in his late teens, a dropout, the other by his mother.

> No. I didn't talk it over with my mother. She doesn't care whether I go to school or not. We don't talk about things like that.

> I didn't say anything to him. I don't know about school. He says it's hard. He says he is too old. He says he can get a job without it. I don't know. I wanted him to go on, but I didn't like to talk about it.

When an Indian student is much older than his classmates, he may feel embarrassed, an additional excuse for dropping out. If age is the only reason for leaving school, a satisfactory change to an Indian boarding school may provide an opportunity to continue education without feeling out of place. However, all the students I talked to who had attended both boarding schools and public schools thought that they obtained a better education at public school. Indian boarding schools function as a sort of threat to the children. A particularly troublesome child is usually sent off to one of the boarding schools, and thus, education is used as a form of punishment and the school is a kind of jail.

Of the eight high school graduates at Big Cypress in 1965, five were girls. More girls graduate than boys, and even among those who do not graduate, girls complete more years than the boys. The reason the boys give most frequently for dropping out is that no better jobs are available with a diploma than without one. The second most commonly given answer to the question is that they do not like school. "Boys feel like they're all caged up in something when they go to school." I asked how school could be made more attractive, especially to the boys.

> It would help if there were more books for older people at the (Big Cypress) school, and have it open like a library, instead of those first and second grade books they have over there. They have some older books, but mostly for the first and second grades.

> The people at the agency and school encourage boys to stay in school, but they could do more. They don't show how it is better for them to stay in school. It helps you get better jobs and get better along in life.

> I don't think anyone can do anything. We have to stay in until we are sixteen, but after that I'm going. I don't like school and I don't think anyone can change that.

Girls on the other hand seem to like school. They also express greater expectation of future employment using their education as secretaries or possibly nurses. The tribe employs a number of Indian women in a secretarial capacity at Hollywood, although the women must live there because the distance is too great to commute. However, the precedent for employment does exist for educated women, while there is none for men.

The tribal leaders have encouraged the young people to stay in school, but even the leaders do not make any forceful effort to affect the individual's thinking. The leaders are a product of the tradition of individual autonomy, and are reluctant to appear to be interferring with other people's affairs. One of the leaders has spoken in favor of business school for the high school graduates, for he would like to see some of the young people trained in areas which could help the tribal enterprises. But even his encouragement has been in the form of gentle suggestions rather than powerful persuasion. He too does not wish to intrude upon the privacy of others. He can see an immediate use for business training, but he thinks that a general college degree would be less valuable for Big Cypress students at this time.

Educated Indians returning to live on the reservations should be a source of encouragement to young people in school. But all too frequently they do not go back after completing advanced work. They may go back to visit, but they do not go back to live. Some tribes, recognizing the problem of the "brain drain," have made scholarships contingent upon a promise to return to the reservation for a stipulated period after the degree has been attained. There are several reasons why the educated Indian remains off the reservation: lack of suitable employment opportunities, lack of any traditional status for the educated Indian, unsatisfactory relationships with reservation Indians of the same age, boredom on the reservation, and the absence of intellectual and social pleasures to which the individual had become accustomed while away at school.

During my years of study at Big Cypress, only one Indian finished advanced work. She has already been mentioned as the first manager of the new store at Big Cypress. Her comments about her life at Big Cypress after she returned point up clearly some of the problems.

> There are people on the reservation who don't seem to like me. Maybe they are jealous, but I don't know why. I know they resent me somehow.
>
> It was hard for me to get used again to the way people talk. They have nothing interesting to talk about. They gossip.
>
> And it was hard getting used to what people think about time. You know, when you live in the city and work, everything is according to time. You race yourself to death really. But I got use to that. But here when you want something done, people take their time doing things. They don't come to work when they should. You are being paid for a certain performance. If you do not do what you are supposed to, you do not get paid. But how do I get that across to the people?
>
> I was lonely when I first came back here. I was ready to pack up and go back. People hardly talked to me . . . just a few words to me.
>
> My idea was that being raised on the reservation, I could see the problems here and also I hoped in the future the girls here would come to me and ask about what they could do after they finished high school. I thought they would discuss their problems to me, what their goals should be. I'd be happy to talk with them. But I myself cannot go to them and tell them what to do.
>
> Some of them start calling me bossy. But that is my responsibility. I tried to talk to them and tell them why I wanted them to come to work on time, but still they didn't. I want them to realize that they had to work to earn their money. It is not a gift. They are supposed to do something in return for their wages.
>
> If I didn't have a family here, it would be almost like going to live with strangers.

Motivation to return to the reservation depends on some sort of reward expectations. This woman expected to contribute to the young people by counseling and advice. However, she found that her expectations of behavior differed from the expectations of the other Indians. The lack of predictable role behavior made relationships very tentative and fragile, and far from being sought out, she was actually isolated from the very age group she hoped to influence.

Although a few older people have expressed an interest in the possibility of adult classes, there is no program of adult education at present. There are two men who show interest and aptitude in auto mechanics; they would like to operate a service station on the reservation. However, they have no conception of difficulties they would encounter, for they believe that the ability and interest developed in tinkering is all the training required to repair any sort of automobile. Without some education the men would not even be able to order parts and supplies or even give proper instructions to any English-speaking secretary who might order for them. They do not have a grasp of the problem, nor do they understand the importance of finely machined parts and the need for extreme accuracy for repairs on piston rings or valves, for example. Whether an adult education program could supply this lack is questionable, but in any business or service organization which the Indians might see as an economic possibility, education, or rather the lack of it, stands as a barrier.

Various state and county extension services are available to the Indians, but these services hardly qualify as adult education. A home demonstrator goes to Big Cypress regularly to show the women how to use ovens to bake, and to teach them about such things as insecticides, detergents, scouring powders, floor waxes, and to impart other information to new owners of the CBS homes who have no experience in the upkeep of a house. The county sanitarian gives lectures on sanitation from time to time. Or there may be a lecture on the care and use of guns. Agricultural agents give advice on the cattle program, but useful though all of this information doubtless is, it does not supply the literacy or skills which are necessary to most employment.

There are problems concerning instructional materials unique to Indian schools. I looked at the textbooks used to teach reading to the first graders and found titles as *Reading Skill,* and *Diagnostic Reading Readiness Workbook.* In addition, there were many readers and sets of books like the Dick and Jane primers. All of these books are highly regarded by educators in the general society, but many of them are far from suitable for teaching reservation Indian children. They depend upon pictorial stimulation whereby the illustration on each page tells a story which is summed up in a brief sentence. "Oh, funny Dick." "See Spot." Many of the pictures have no meaning for Indian children, especially for the children at Big Cypress. Although intended to portray common childhood experiences, many of the illustrations are of activities or items which the Indian children have never heard of, i.e., snow, sleds, snowmen, milkmen, fireplaces. It might be pointed out that although many other children in south Florida have never seen snow, it is nevertheless a part of their cultural background. One Indian child asked me to tell him about snow. It was very difficult for me, and I am not sure that he believed me. I made analogies to ice cream and the frost inside the freezers at the store, but I have a distinct impression that he did not really get the idea at all.

In addition to items which may be considered regional, there are relationships pictured which are largely meaningless to Indian children. Here I refer not only to the different relationship the people in the outside culture have with animals as pets, but also to the expression of family affection such as hugging and kissing, which until recently were not done at Big Cypress.

> In all my life I never saw my daddy hug my mother before my eyes, and I've never been kissed by either of them as far as I can remember. Now you see it on TV, and it seems natural there. My sister or brother bring their kids over and maybe we kiss them on the face, but when we were kids it was different. My father never kissed me.

> The first time I saw a mother kiss her child, it was when I went to school in Clewiston. It made me sort of sick.

A speech therapist comes to the reservation school on certain days to help the children with their English pronunciation. They have most difficulty learning to make the *th* sound because it does not occur in Mikasuki. *Father* comes out *fodder*. The teachers also teach the children hygiene. The children brush their teeth and wash their hands and comb their hair at school. Combs, brushes, toothbrushes, and toothpaste are all supplied to the children by the government. Sometimes the Indian teacher's aide plays beauty parlor with the girls. One child is selected, and the aide combs and arranges her hair and cuts and cleans her fingernails. Hygiene is also taught in movies on dental care, germs, and disease. The children are even shown how to use and flush a toilet.

Materials for the arts and crafts periods are plentiful: clay, paints, crayons, chalk, paste, colored paper, felts, pipe cleaners—just about everything. In the summer school art and craft sessions, some quite elaborate work is produced, and there is a show for the parents at the end of the term. For summer school there are no report cards, either for the academic activities or for the crafts. The children progress at their own speed. Recorded music, particularly folk music, is played during the craft sessions.

A summer sewing clinic is held for teenage girls. Before the new school was built, the sewing clinic was held in the recreation hall. Seminole girls have learned to do traditional sewing on the electric portable machines or the hand-operated machines by the time they are about ten years old, but they have not learned to use patterns or to follow fitting instructions. When they start the girls assume that they know all there is to know about sewing because they have been making Seminole skirts for so long. They work too fast and ignore instructions with the result that they have to rip out a lot of seams. But it is not long before they realize the advantages of using patterns and fitting the clothes to the individual. Under the guidance of a government supplied teacher, they are soon turning out well made garments.

The government has sewing machines delived to the school, where they are available for the girls during the three week period. There are enough machines so that there is no waiting. Some of the girls are cutting, fitting, or hand fiinishing while others are using the machines. The government also supplies all the cotton material the girls can use in the three weeks. Most of the girls turn out six to ten skirts, but some work on more difficult patterns of dresses, suits, and shorts. Those eligible are limited to girls who will be in school in September, and the summer sewing session is the most important source of clothing for the school girls.

# Religion

Big Cypress has a church operated as part of the Baptist Home Missions. Although not all Mikasuki are Christians, most of the residents at one time or another attend the services or meetings in the church. There are monthly Sunday night suppers which are important to the older men and women of the the reservation, and a group of women meets regularly as the Women's Missionary Society. The missionary who lives at Hollywood conducts occasional services at Big Cypress, but most of the services are conducted in Mikasuki by men of the reservation who are deacons in the church. One man has started his own church on the reservation, but his attendance is largely limited to relatives.

Until 1967 a bible school was operated during the daytime in the summer, but with the increased attendance of children at Headstart and other government summer school programs, the bible school hours were changed to the evening to avoid conflict.

The pulpit is used to make announcements of all political meetings and elections, statements of who is running, places and times, and so on, but not for any campaigning. Political speeches are saved for meetings at the school or the wood-shop. The church building is used for announcements because it is there that the largest congregation of people may be reached at one time. Besides functioning in this fashion, appeals are often made to the membership for contributions to hardship cases on the reservation.

In general the religious approach is not to introduce practical solutions to problems on the reservation or to encourage school attendance or job perseverence. Rather it is an appeal for personal salvation and redemption. Save your soul, enter heaven. It is an appeal to personal security in an afterlife, and good deeds should be done for this end or to convert others. There is no systematic attempt to analyze and solve the problems of daily life.

Swanton (1925a:478 *et seq.*) gives us a general statement about the aboriginal belief systems of all the southeastern Indians. It was belived that the world was flat and over it the stars, moon, and sun were stuck on the vault of the sky. The Creek Indians had names for some of the constellations. The Great Dipper was called the image of a canoe, the galaxy was the spirits road, and supernaturals lived on the sun and moon. A big frog swallowing the moon produced lunar eclipses. The rainbow was called the cutter of the rain and was thought to be a huge snake. Beyond these beliefs, Christian teachings are so entwined that it is impossible to distinguish what may be precontact. For instance, it is probably Christian influence when there is reference to good souls and bad souls going to different regions after death. It is also impossible to say whether there was an aboriginal concept of a high god or supreme good spirit. Such references by early writers are probably their own attempts to squeeze Indian religious beliefs into prior European categories. I give below one Indian's cosmology. It is representative of belief at Big Cypress whether or not the individual is a member of the local church. I could find no one who remembered any beliefs untouched by the various versions of Christianity.

Swanton (1925a:483) reported the following to demonstrate how Christian belief has obscured Indian belief. It was told to him by an old informant who had been born in Alabama before the migration to Oklahoma.

This man said that a child was born in a certain country and a time came in the history of those people when children were to be killed. Rather than lose their child its parents put it into a basket, pitched it with gum, and set it afloat upon the water. Afterwards it was seen by the king, who told an attendant to bring it in, and he did so. Fascinated by its beauty he adopted it and reared it. One day after he grew up this child was walking along and saw a man planting seed. He asked him what it was and the man answered, "I am planting stones." Later he went to his place again, dug into the earth, and found a great many stones there. Another time when he met this man the latter had some white corn flour. He threw a handful of this into the air and it turned into white water herons found along streams, the feathers of which were used in the Creek peace dance. The old man said that the man who did this was Christ and added that "a darn Frenchman came along and killed him."

Since Swanton collected this story more than fifty years ago and even then came to the conclusion that it was clearly taken from the story of Moses, I recognized the improbability of recording any aboriginal or precontact beliefs or legends. Nevertheless, I asked an old medicine man in his ninth decade of life to tell me the Seminole beliefs about the origins of man and the world. I thought if anyone remembered old legends it would surely be he. I got this response.

God (*Fishakikomechi* in Mikasuki) created the world. Before that it was just water. God put animals and plants on the soil. Then he made a man he called Adam. At first Adam was the only person and he got lonely. So God created a woman and called her Eve. There was one plant that Adam and Eve could not eat. But there was a snake that told Eve it was all right to eat the plant. Eve gave it to the man, and he ate it. Then the man and woman knew they were naked, so they hid because it was not right. Then they made clothes from large leaves. They had children of all different colors and that is how there got to be so many different people in the world. But after while there was too much drinking and too many wives. So Noah built a boat and got some animals and people to live on the boat with him. Then water came over the land and people who didn't have boats were drowned. After the water went down the people went back to the land to live. They had lots of children. Jesus came and preached around, but some people hated him and killed him. Jesus arose and went to his followers and they all had a feast with wine. Jesus said that since people had killed him he wasn't going to live on this land and had to go back to heaven. Jesus taught the people how to grow corn first. This is a story I heard from my grandfather, "He-who-forgets-his-language," The Stutterer.

This same medicine man, when asked if there were any people who could practice witchcraft, replied in the affirmative and volunteered the information that he had a picture of one. I was fascinated and asked him to show it to me. He disappeared into his chickee returning in a short time with a copy of the *Golden Book of Indian Crafts and Lore.* In it he pointed to a picture of a Mohawk warrior.

# 5

# Social Organization

## Marriage and the Family

THE FAMILY IS THE GROUP to which the Mikasuki feel primary allegiance. At Big Cypress today the family is either nuclear or matrilineal extended in structure, and there is a growing trend toward recognition of the nuclear family as the most important social group. A matrilineal extended family typically might consist of a husband and wife, their unmarried sons and daughters, their married daughters and husbands, grandchildren, perhaps aged or dependent individuals of the wife's clan, and maybe some orphans of that clan group. The ties between mother, father, and minor children seem to be more enduring now than ties between either parent and his or her natal family. The bond between mother and children is far stronger than the marriage bond, the fragility of which is indicated by the large number of unstable unions. While a child is recognized as being equally related to both mother and father, he usually feels closer to relatives on the maternal side.

In 1964 there were three marriages at Big Cypress which were initiated by state civil ceremonies. In each case the legal marriage was necessary to ensure the adoption or guardianship of minor children. The rest of the marriages have been either traditional, an agreement between families and arranged by elders, or a more recent form of marriage in which the couple concerned simply live with each other and declare themselves married. Swanton (1928:376) describes traditional marriage form.

> The official marriage in the case of young people is made for, not by, them. It represents the kind of union which agrees with tribal convention and ought to be best for the prosperity of the clans concerned, and for the couple so married. The parties thus mated are of the proper clans, the proper standing in the tribe, the proper age, and their virtues are such as to constitute a fair exchange.

Swanton adds that couples did not always get along, and divorce was frequent. Liaisons or attachments were allowed as long as they were not incestuous or

adulterous. Today many marriages are not announced until pregnancy occurs. The state of Florida recognizes Indian unions as a form of legal common law marriage. However, the state and federal officials have been increasingly concerned about the problems of child support, inheritance, and wife support and have urged civil ceremonies to make clear the legal responsibilities and rights of marriage. The agency mimeographed a booklet, "Let's Get Married," which explains how to get a blood test, marriage license, and where to go for the ceremony. It also attempts to outline the responsibilities of marriage.

There are no polygynous marriages now, but the practice has been recent enough so that even the adolescents can remember when some men had more than one wife. One man who was alive at the time Nash visited Big Cypress in 1930 had had at least five wives, some say seven. This individual was very old then, and all his wives had died, but the instance demonstrates that polygyny was practiced within the last few decades. Where polygyny existed, the wives were usually sisters, although there are known cases of nonrelated co-wives. In the latter case they had separate dwellings.

When a couple marries now the man may move to the household of the girl's parents, the couple may establish a camp of their own, or they may spend only nights together at the camp of parents on either side, and live and eat apart most of the time. The reason for this last practice is economic, the man being employed off the reservation or lacking enough money to construct a camp of his own. The couple usually expects to build a camp when they can afford it. The ideal, according to young people, is a camp of their own, perhaps some day a real house, although not all the young couples perfer a house over the traditional chickee.

There are frequent changes in residence. These changes involve moves from camp to camp as well as destinations off the reservation. Nevertheless at the time these data were gathered, there were 19 camps of nuclear families, 13 of matri-lineal extended families, 6 camps occupied by single individuals, 4 camps composed of people related in the second or third degree, 3 camps where a bride had gone to live with her husband's family, and 7 households of women related through the agnatic line. Residence, therefore, is largely opportunistic. One lives where there is room, where the people are compatible, and where it is economically wise.

A young man, it is said, was once expected to marry a much older woman for his first wife, and there are many marriages today in which the woman is older, one case by 15 years, one by 10. However, now that virtually no marriages are arranged by the families of the spouses, the young people tend to choose mates close to their own age. Some people say that the wife should be older than man so that she can teach him and provide a stabilizing influence. Others say that it is bad to have spouses close in age because they become too sexually interested in each other and such things are "not right." Some older people also said that it was once common for a young girl to be married to a much older man so that he could teach her, but there are no marriages today where the man is much older than the woman. In most marriages the woman is slightly older. Age plays little part in the selection of a mate; qualities of even temper and competence are far more important.

Racially mixed marriages occur, most frequently with Mexican or Puerto Rican men living on the plantations surrounding the reservation. There are also a number of half white children whose parents never married. In 1964 there were 7 women out of a total of 42 between the ages of 18 and 50 who had borne 8 children fathered by men other than their husbands, and there were 14 children born to 8 women who had never been married at the time the children were born. Most of these children are racially mixed. There were frequent Indian-Negro marriages long ago when the Indians owned Negro slaves, and there have been a few more recent Negro-Indian marriages. It is a tribal law that no non-Indian man can live on the reservation. Consequently, since all of these mixed marriages involved Indian women and non-Indian men, many of the women moved off the reservation to live, returning for periodic visits.

There was one marriage between an Indian man and a Spanish woman (she was probably Mexican, but the Indians called her Spanish because she spoke that language). He brought her to the reservation to live, but many of the Indian women and men did not approve, partly because she was an outsider, partly because he had deserted an Indian wife to take a new spouse.

The attitudes toward mixed marriage are noticeably different from those MacCauley (1884:479) reports. He counted three Negro wives and seven Negro-Indian children. He said:

> Their sexual morality is a matter of common notoriety. The white half-breed does not exist among the Florida Seminole, and nowhere could I learn that the Seminole woman is other than virtuous and modest. The birth of a white half-breed would be followed by the death of the Indian mother at the hands of her own people.

In 1930, by contrast, Nash (1931:24) reports at least three half white children and says that two Seminole women were prostitutes. He does not say whether those women were Muskogee or Mikasuki. In the mid-1960s there were in Big Cypress four children of an Indian mother and white father who had been married by a state ceremony. The mother had left her husband and returned to Big Cypress with the children. As already noted, there are some other racially mixed families living in Immokalee. One family at Big Cypress claims to have had a Chinese ancestor.

The concept of physical attractiveness seems to play no part in the selection of a spouse. The ideal man should be a good hunter, like children, help around the camp, and not get drunk. The ideal wife should be a good cook, not talk too much, never nag or scold, and sew well. Physical attributes are never mentioned. A good disposition is the primary quality which both sexes seek.

Divorce is frequent and easy. It may be accomplished by desertion, by mutual consent, or by legal state divorce. All divorced people except one man and one woman have remarried. The reasons given for divorce are few: women usually want to marry someone else or have already begun living with someone else; the men report that they did not want to support so many children so they abandoned them, or they say that they disliked their wives because they were bad tempered. One woman claimed she left her husband because he beat her. She then went to live with a man who she described as "dumb but very kind."

Nash (1931:26) quotes a 1915 annual report to the Commissioner of Indian Affairs which said that there was only one divorced couple among *all* Seminole. This statement must be regarded with some suspicion, and one wonders what means was used to ascertain the divorce rate. Anyone asking a question of how many divorces there were would probably have been told that there were none, or not many, for that is what is said today. Yet a more careful investigation shows that there are 17 camps where divorced people are living, and there must have been more than 17 divorces since some of these people have been divorced several times. Changes in marriage stability have not been marked during the last century. Divorce is very easy, and it has been easy for a long time; besides, no one keeps divorce statistics. As far as the time depth of high divorce rates is concerned, MacCauley (1884:497) observed in 1880 that, "In fact, marriage among these Indians seems to be but the natural mating of the sexes, to cease at the option of either of the interested parties." In other words, MacCauley's observation supports the present contention that divorce is frequent and easy. On this basis we may conclude that the significant change has not been in the divorce rate, but in the breakdown of the clan which was responsible for the children who were the products of a broken marriage. The lack of a clan group to absorb children of broken marriages makes divorce seem more common than before. The children still stay with their mother in almost every case, but the mother no longer has the support of an organized group to help her feed and clothe them. If she does not marry again, she must go on relief. That is in fact what has happened to one Big Cypress family in which a divorced mother with seven children has not remarried.

Fostering is common. Couples who have no children of their own will often take a relative's child, particularly if the relative has a large family or if the child was born out of wedlock. Old people whose children have grown up and left home will sometimes take a grandchild to raise, and the child will stay with the grandparents until adulthood. A structural situation more closely resembling adoption has occurred in two cases. Without recourse to state courts, two couples adopted children and gave the children their name. There is only one child on the reservation who was legally adopted; the other two cases mentioned may be considered *de facto* adoption in terms of social recognition by the community members. All the adopted children know that they are adopted. They also know who their real parents (or at least their mothers) are and most of them visit the biological parents from time to time. An adopted child retains the clan membership of his genetic mother. He does not under any circumstances take on the clan of the adoptive mother.

## The Camp

The camp is the residential unit, and "camp" means both the members of the household and the site. The number of occupants of the camps ranged from 1 to 13 in 1964. The physical elements of the camp have changed very little since MacCauley visited the Seminole in 1880, but the small birth chickee and the seclusion chickee for menstuating women are no longer present. Babies today are born in the hospital and menstruating women are no longer segregated. When the camp is occupied by a matrilineal extended family, each nuclear family has its own sleeping chickee. When an extended family moves into a cement block structure, each nuclear family gets a bedroom, one of which may actually have been intended as the living room.

The camps today are permanent. The temporary camps used by hunting parties in the past are rarely built because the hunters make part of their trip by truck and return home to sleep. During the vegetable growing season, some people leave their Big Cypress camps and go to Immokalee to work. There is a camp area in Immokalee where Indians have built chickees in which they live when working on the ranches or at the shipping depots. A few Indian women live in Immokalee permanently with their non-Indian husbands because these men are not allowed to live at Big Cypress.

The number of nuclear families constituting the entire camp has increased to almost half the total number of camps. This trend is probably a consistent one, which means that the extended family grouping will eventually disappear. In terms of modernization, the extended family is particularly awkward for domicile in a Western style house. When an additional chickee could be raised with little effort, new units to the camp caused no stress, but the crowding of an extended family into a nonexpandible cement block building puts a strain on all the inhabitants.

The camp is the basic economic unit in the society. There may be one kitchen chickee in which all the women prepare food, but after it is prepared, it is taken by each woman to her own chickee. Anyone living in the camp, however, feels free to help himself to food at any chickee without an invitation. There seems to be no regularity in financial contribution to the common larder, but it is said that there is sharing within the camp if food is in short supply. People cannot imagine that one family should eat while others go hungry.

## Behavior Patterns

Parent-child relationships are marked by a definite discontinuity in most families. Babies of both sexes are loved and handled almost constantly not only by parents and older siblings, but by anyone visiting the household. The usual treatment is one of indulgence until the baby walks. At that time he is most frequently handed over to an older sibling or relative for his daily care, and the mother spends very little time with the child from then on. This is especially true if the mother works in the fields or if, as often happens, there is a new baby. In contrast to babyhood's warm attentions, the child is often ignored even when he misbehaves. By the time a child reaches adolescence, most parents refuse to interfere in any way with his behavior. This indifference may be present even when the child's activities are dangerous to himself or to others. It is not unusual to see a barefoot child play with an empty cola bottle, break it, and continue to play until he is rather badly cut. The mother will then remove the broken glass and care for the child, but often the child gets another bottle and plays with it.

It should not be assumed that parents do not love their children after babyhood, but there are no approved methods of chastising children since the

*A typical camp of Chickees.*

*Seminole baby with dress in traditional style.*

traditional punishment of scratching miscreants with garfish jaws or needles has been abolished. Long ago, it is said, a child who was scratched by his mother's brother was very ashamed of the scars and almost never misbehaved again. One informant said, "All we can do with naughty children is tell them that they won't go to Jesus when they die." This threat of delayed punishment does not carry much deterrent force. A few parents spank children, although most say that this kind of punishment is not a good thing and should be avoided. The idea of reasoning with children or trying to discuss behavior problems with them has apparently never occurred to parents. One informant who had left Big Cypress to go to school said that if she could tell Indians at home just one thing it would be, "Talk to each other. Try to understand each other." She thought that a lack of communication between the generations was the most serious problem at Big Cypress. Certainly observation indicates that problem-solving communication is at a minimum among adults, and between adults and adolescents it is almost non-existent. For example, a boy in his late teens dropped out of school, although his academic performance had been highly satisfactory. He left school because he felt out of place with all his classmates considerably younger than he was. When the teacher suggested that he talk his problem over with his parents before his final decision, he said, "I don't talk about things like that to my family." The teacher tried to persuade his mother to urge him to stay in school, but she said, "I don't tell him what to do," and refused to discuss the matter further. This situation has its counterpart in child-parent relationships in almost every family. One student commented to me. "Some parents never talk to their children at all. They don't even know that children have different problems from what the parents had when they were children." It appeared to me, however, that the parents did recognize that the experiences of the children were vastly different from their own at that age. It was precisely this recognition which made parents reluctant to give advice, for they felt inadequately prepared to help.

Mothers teach their daughters traditional tasks, like sewing the strips, but not many girls are accomplished in the traditional sewing. They now prefer to make clothes that are fashionable according to the taste of the general population. Boys are still taken hunting by fathers, uncles or elder brothers, but in general children do less and less in the company of their parents. Most education of the young now comes from school, and very few parents can help their children in matters of formal education, for very few adults can read or write. The children respect their parents, but after babyhood, the outward manifestation of the relationship between the generations is indifference and distance. Siblings of the same sex and good friends share a much closer relationship than parents and their children. In fact, the most intimate feelings are between friends and siblings of the same sex. This intimacy does not appear to be a common revolt against parental authority, but rather the result of sharing similar problems and similar aspirations, neither of which are the same as those of the people in the parents' generation.

While there is no talk of school problems or jobs, there is still an intimacy between mothers and their daughters in the form of education about sex and the body functions. Reproduction and other biological facts are openly discussed among the women and girls as perfectly normal occurrences, although one informant reported that her mother was embarrassed by the "facts of life" and refused to discuss sex with her. The girl believed that her mother thought "sex was dirty," and the girl was disturbed that she could not be frank with her mother.

It appeared to me that the sister-sister relationship was the strongest kin relationship. Sisters are often their own best friends, turning to each other for advice and comfort. The brother-sister bond is affectionate and often an almost joking relationship, although it tends to be individualistic rather than culturally patterned. Another strong and fond tie exists between the maternal aunt and her sisters' children, especially the daughters. Mother's sisters are always available for help and counsel unless separated geographically. The father-son or father-daughter relationship is, by contrast, one of respect which varies considerably depending upon the individuals involved. However, it is generally correct to say that it is not as abiding or close as the others mentioned.

In none of these relationships is there a real authority structure after the child has reached adolescence. Even within the family, individual autonomy is the respected norm. One may give advice, but not a command. One teenage boy whose parents keep close watch over him and control his life carefully is both pitied and ridiculed by his peers. People say that his mother guards him too closely. "Some day he will break away." It is implied that the break away will be violent. Children approaching adulthood are supposed to think for themselves. It is expected that they may make a few mistakes, but they will not only be forgiven, they will even learn through their mistakes. It is a common phrase, "We all make mitsakes." There will inevitably be gossip, but in a little while everyone will stop talking and soon they will all forget. The basic strength of the sibling tie is such that it endures through time, strife, and all the strain that individuality can bring to bear. What the individual does is his own business. It reflects neither glory nor shame on his family. There is no pressure to uphold the family honor. Just as one's mistakes are one's own and rather soon forgotten, so one's success is one's own. Relatives, even close relatives, do not bask in reflected glory. This is not to say that family members do not care about each other or do not feel sad when misfortune strikes, but rather that one person cannot bring either dishonor or distinction to the others. Thus brothers feel no responsibility to guard their sister's chastity or to force shotgun marriages. It is sister's business and brother will not interfere.

Any culturally specialized behavior patterns between relatives other than parent-child and sibling-sibling have disappeared. Those existing are completely individualistic. Children have heard that mother's brother use to be the authority, but he no longer has such a position. There is total disagreement even among older people about respect and joking relations. Everyone says something different except that there is general agreement concerning the expectation that all young people should respect all old people. There never have been avoidance customs that anyone remembers, and questions about joking behavior elicit as much variety in answer as questions about respect. Completely contradictory statements are given. Thus, "You should show respect to members of your own clan and joke with members of your father's clan," and "You should respect all people in your father's clan and joke with members of your own clan" were statements gathered on joking relations, and no discernable majority of informants favor one such statement over the other.

The husband-wife relationship is one of equality. Wives do not feel inferior because they are women. The female sex is not considered inferior to the male, merely different and complementary. There are reports of wife beating by inebriated husbands, and there are reports of shrewish wives and henpecked husbands. At one election it was all the officials could do to restrain a wife from entering the polling booth with the husband "to be sure he voted right." The complementarity of the husband-wife relationship lies in the division of labor. Women take care of the home and raise the children; men hunt or go to work and support the family. This is the ideal that is still expressed, even though women are just as frequently employed in cash work as the men. No one ever suggests that the wife should obey her husband or be in subjugation to him. Such a value or norm does not exist in Mikasuki society. The children are not raised to think of the father as "boss" or the mother as subservient to him. As a matter of fact, once there are children, many wives tend to "take over" and more or less run the family. At this point the husband/father may escape to purely masculine society in hunting or drinking. Women's aggression appears as a result of motherhood and protectiveness toward the offspring.

The relation between husband and wife differs somewhat depending upon the ages of the spouses. Younger married couples are in many respect the duplicate of their counterpart in the general American population. For these young people there is a romantic element to marriage, and they spend a lot of their leisure time together. Besides this they plan the future together, do their shopping together, and travel together within and outside the reservation. On the other hand, older people spend far more time apart than together. Women associate with women, and men with men. The women take care of children and housework while the men are usually away hunting, working, or just visiting. Overt indications of affection are considered improper and do not occur even among the younger couples. This particular lack of Western orientation may be seen in their attitude toward kissing, which is considered little short of disgusting.

One hears of wife beating and shrewish women, but to ears attuned to our own noisy society, married life among the Mikasuki seems quiet and calm indeed. One reason that violent arguments are not common may result from the fact that the relationship can so easily be changed if it does not prove satisfactory, that is, the ease of divorce makes patient endurance unnecessary.

The ease of divorce also produces a multiplicity of in-laws and step-parents, and in a group as small as this one any avoidance of people in these categories would be impossible. These relationships, in-law/in-law and step-parent/step-child, like most other kin relationships are unpatterned and depend upon the individuals involved. Generally step-parents are not close to their step-children whereas foster parents and their adopted children have as close a relationship as do natural parents with their children. The abvious reason for the difference in the case of fostering children is that there was mutual choice or that the child was taken so young that the foster parent relationship is the only one known. In the case of the step-parent, the new parent is assuming the role of a remembered and loved person, usually without any consultation with the children. It is not a mutual choice, but rather looked upon as usurpation. It is therefore likely to be a very fragile relationship. Relatives by marriage are not counted intimate members of the family unless the in-marrying individual, on a purely individual basis, is so well liked that he makes his own special relationships with his affines. "He is married to my aunt," is the expression of the relationship rather than "He is my uncle," or "He is my uncle by marriage." In-laws do not fall into any incest prohibition category, nor do step-children. To marry a step-child is rare, but it has happened within the past generation.

# The Clan

The Seminole follow the typical southeastern pattern of descent, counting it through the female line. Although equality of relatives on both maternal and paternal sides is recognized, and although there is no longer any authority pattern maintained, the system cannot be considered bilateral because for marriage allocation clan membership is still important. Every individual on the reservation knows the clan membership of every other. When asked why he did not consider a particular girl as a possible wife, a young man replied, "I can't. She's my kinfolk." The girl was a member of his clan, and therefore she could not be considered a marriage partner even though she was from one of the other reservations.

There are only seven clans represented at Big Cypress now: Tiger, Wind, Bird, Otter, Bear, Wolf, and Big Town. "Tiger" is really an incorrect translation of the Mikasuki word which means puma, an animal native to the southeastern area, for the tiger is an Asiatic or African animal. However, most published material on the Seminole uses the term "Tiger," and the Big Cypress people translate the word as "Tiger," so that practice will be followed here rather than chance confusion. Two of the clans, the Bear and the Wolf, are becoming extinct. The four members of the Bear clan (three old men and one childless old woman) are without issue that would satisfy traditional criteria for clan membership, and the only Wolf left is an old man. Furthermore, adoption to prevent clan extinction is impossible since a child retains the clan of his genetic mother under all circumstances including adoption.

The clan is not a corporate body. There is no longer any acknowledged clan head nor are there meetings of clansmen. The ceremonial Green Corn Dance which was organized along clan lines is no longer held at Big Cypress. With its disappearance went the last social or ritual season for collective activity by the clans. The main function of the clan today is to regulate marriage, for clan exogamy is still observed. To marry within one's own clan is thought to be bad, even though there are four intraclan marriages in the community at present. The people in these marriages are not outcasts in any way, but everyone knows that they have broken clan exogamy, and it is spoken of very disapprovingly. However, among the younger adults there is some sentiment that the clan system is an irrational way to choose mates. One informant said,

> Clans are silly for marriage regulations. First cousins are not necessarily in the clan, but some are. We can't marry some, but we can marry the others. They are all the same in closeness. Some people say that is why _____'s little boy is not right, because she and her husband are too closely related. Clans don't take care of that.

Some Big Cypress people think that cousin marriage results in sick or retarded children.

In the strict sense of the word, none of the clans is totemic, the members do not claim to be descendants of an animal, nor is there any sort of taboo against killing or eating the eponym. Big Town was a late development to absorb non-Indian women into the system. The origin myth of this clan has several versions, but they all involve foreign females coming to live with the Seminole and being allocated to this clan. One old informant said that Big Town was ranked below all other clans, but there is no indication that members of the Big Town clan feel themselves to be inferior. The alleged racial mixture which is supposed to have occurred in absorbing non-Indian women into Big Town clan is no more apparent in this group than among the rest of the society as a whole.

There was at one time a moiety division, but only the old people remember it. When the people used to assemble for the Green Corn Dance (the Busk of the southeastern Indians), they divided into two groups which sat in a semicircle around the dance fire, members of the head clan of each moiety opposite each other. The members of the head clan of the moiety were referred to and addressed by the other moiety members as mother's brother.

The two clans which provided moiety heads were Tiger and Wind, and origin myths have these two clans coming into existence almost simultaneously. It is said that the moieties were once exogamous, but if that were so, it changed long ago. On a practical demographic level, the population has been too small since the end of the Third Seminole War to maintain that type of exogamy. Some people still acknowledge the members of one clan as mother's brothers to their own, but only old people know that this was once accompanied by exogamy. MacCauley (1884:507) says that a member of the Wind clan told him that clans were graded in the following order. (Big Town is not mentioned by MacCauley.)

1. Wind
2. Tiger
3. Otter
4. Bird
5. Deer
6. Snake
7. Bear
8. Wolf

If there ever had been ranking of the clans, Tiger and Wind probably would have been the highest, although this is surmise since there seems to be no ranking now. Speaking of Creek social organization, from which the Seminole was derived, Swanton (1925a:167) says, "Some of the small clans were regarded as inferiors by the others, and this may have been due in some cases to a slave origin. . . ." The factor of slave origin may have been involved in Seminole clan ranking also, but there is no way to demonstrate that possibility. People on the reservation seemed surprised when I asked if the clans were ranked. One woman said:

> I have always been proud to be a Bird because I think that is better than a Tiger or Otter or something. Birds are nice. But I don't think anyone else thinks that way. I guess everyone thinks his own clan is best. I never heard that anyone is ashamed of his clan.

The most significant change in social organization has been the attenuation of clan authority. Traditionally these groups exercised extensive social control over the lives of their members. For example, boys and young men were punished by the clan elders by the traditional scratching. Severity and extent of scratching depended upon the magnitude of the infractions of the law. However, even when the scratches were relatively mild, scars remained long enough for all to see, and it was a humiliating experience.

The elder clansmen also punished adulterers and those who had committed incest by cutting off the noses, ears, and lips of the offenders and occasionally decreeing a penalty of death. Today, however, clans are noncorporate groups whose only function is the regulation of marriage through the observance of clan exogamy, and even this observance is weakening.

Among the pre-Columbian Creek, each town had a leader who was called *Micco.* He was supported and advised by an official entourage of retainers and a body of retired warriors who formed a council. The Micco was a civilian leader, and in times of war, a war chief was chosen to command. The war chief was expected to have attained his position by prowess and also through the help of visions promising aid from the spirit world. The Micco always came from one moiety and the war chief from the other. These divisions have been called "The White People, The People of Peace" and the "Red People, The People of Alien Speech" or "War People." The Europeans came and disrupted the whole system before the arrangement was completely worked out. The big chief, the Micco, in the traditional system was a position inherited in certain clans. However, the *Tustenugge,* war chief, achieved his position through his ability as a warrior. The clans most frequently producing the Micco when the Mikasuki were still considered part of the Lower Creek are given by Swanton as Alligator or Snake. Swanton reports the second in command, called *Heniha,* to have come from either Alligator or Panther (another translation term for puma). Furthermore, Swanton (1925*a*:192–193) states that the chiefs probably came from different clans in different towns. In other words, the leadership inheritance was not a rigid tradition. The Alligator and Snake clans are extinct at Big Cypress today. Even as early as 1880 MacCauley did not find any Alligator clansmen there. All leaders who arose among the Florida Indians after the Third Seminole War must have been self-made with achieved rather than ascribed positions.

Informants at Big Cypress were unanimous in reporting that their last leaders to inherit positions had come from the Snake clan, and "That was long ago." Even in Swanton's exhaustive discussion of Creek social organization (Swanton 1925*a*) there is much uncertainty about Seminole practices because of their composition as a heterogeneous group, the disturbances of their social structure during the various wars, and their removal to Oklahoma. As customary patterns of social organization were impossible to maintain under the conditions of a half century of warfare, they were abandoned. Indeed in organizational terms it is often difficult to decide what is meant when reading about the "Seminole." Sometimes the word refers to one group at a particular time period, and sometimes to another people and/or another period.

Among the members of the Creek confederacy it was said that,

> the clan [of the chief] would be changed if the tribe suffered any misfortune, or sometimes, as frequently happened in later years, if the royal clan ran out so that

no suitable person could be found in it to occupy the position (Swanton, 1925a: 280–281).

There is no reason to believe that the Mikasuki were any more rigid in these matters. Indeed, considering the size of their population by 1860, they could hardly afford to be. Leaders arising after this period would perforce be leaders on the basis of ability rather than inheritance.

Big Cypress adults today remember that there was a council of elders which functioned as a judiciary and legislative body at the Green Corn Dance. There has been no Green Corn Dance at Big Cypress for about a decade. Anyone wishing to attend one must now go to some other reservation. Nash (1931:26) names four Indians who composed the council in 1930. Two are no longer alive. The remaining two are brothers who were once, before they became Christians, ritual medicine men. It is important to note that the four men did not all belong to the same clan. As far as can be determined by interviews and observation, no one clan has produced the entire leadership during the century.

# Life Cycle

Today all babies are born in the hospital, usually Hendry County Hospital in Clewiston. A few women go to contract doctors in Ft. Lauderdale. During pregnancy the mother is cared for by the county public health nurse and a doctor both under contract to the Bureau of Indian Affairs. The expectant mother is given care that is in every way comparable to that given to the general population, including examinations, tests, and vitamin supplements. Birth control is practiced by some women who take anti-pregnancy pills. Other means of birth control may exist, but were not mentioned by any informants.

Shortly after mother and baby return from the hospital the baby's ears are pierced if it is a girl. Boys no longer have their ears pierced, but there are a number of men who had it done when they were infants. The umbilical cord is allowed to drop off, and some mothers still bury it in a shady spot, although no informant could remember the reason behind this practice. After four moons have passed, the baby has his hair and nails cut. These clippings are saved to give to the child when he is grown. At one time it was believed to be fatal to the baby if his nails were cut before the fourth moon. One baby was brought to the nurse with extensive scratches on his face. As all mothers know, this is common in infancy when the baby flails about in a random fashion and scratches his face in the process. The nurse cut the baby's nails, and not long thereafter the baby died. The mother said it was just a superstition and did not blame the nurse, but since that time the nurse has refused to cut any baby's nails.

The origin and meaning of the practice of saving hair and nail clippings have been forgotten. One woman said she thought it was "just like white people do, like save the baby's shoes." Sometimes a baby garment or two is added to this collection. After the hair cutting ceremony, most babies and mothers have a ritual cold water bath, and then it is considered proper for the mother to sleep with the father again. Traditionally during these four months, the mother and baby lived together in a separate chickee. An old medicine woman, a specialist in female ills, sang songs to make the baby and mother strong. These songs used to be sung just after the mid-wife delivered the baby, and today these songs are still often sung, but after the mother returns from the hospital. The baby's cradle is still the traditional hammock of sturdy white cloth suspended from the rafters of the chickee.

Children are given English names very soon after birth. This practice is the result of pressure to get a name on the birth certificate. Formerly on the fourth day after birth, the baby was given one of a number of Indian names suggested by some old person, the mother choosing the suggested name she preferred. Girls took only one name during their lifetime whereas boys were given a new name at the time of their initiation as hunters during a Green Corn Dance, approximately during their twelfth year. Most Indian children still receive an Indian name during their first week, but in several cases this practice has been dropped. Children now take their last name from their father. Even if the parents are not married, if the father is known, the baby will have his last name.

Babies are nursed or bottle-fed or both. Solids usually partially chewed by the mother are given early, but prepared baby foods are being used with increasing frequency. No two mothers seem to wean babies at the same age, the only custom being that the baby must be weaned from breast feeding if the mother becomes pregnant again. If there are two little children, they are not allowed to drink from the same bottle. Each must have his own. It is believed that to use the same bottle would cause the older child to sicken and die. This belief is probably a carryover from the belief about breast feeding, that is, if two babies were nursed by the same woman, it would be fatal to the older of the two. The most common substitute for breast feeding is evaporated milk, but fresh bottled milk and powdered formula are also used. A few mothers are very careful about boiling the milk and sterilizing the bottles. However, the majority seem to have no worries about such matters. Much of the endemic dysentery and diarrhea could be stopped with better sanitation, and the public health workers are trying hard to improve baby feeding practices and food preservation techniques.

Little children play many games, most of which they have taken over from the dominant American culture. Baseball and basketball are favorites with the older children. The traditional Indian games are no longer played, for very few people under twenty know them. Some of the old people remember playing the Indian form of lacrosse. Boys and girls play together until the boys' voices change; then the sexes usually are separated unless they play an occasional game of softball together. There are no social dances, picnics, organized parties, or systematic dating for the teenagers. Dates are almost clandestine meetings, and there are no courtship activities.

The older women say that when a girl can carry a pail of water, she is old enough to start her education in cooking and housekeeping. It did not appear to me that anyone really expected domestic duties to begin at a special time anymore. Little girls help around the camp almost as soon as they can walk. A boy begins to learn the adult man's ways when he is old enough to shoot a gun. However, as both boys and girls now start school at about age five, there is less and less training in the traditional adult roles. Since the institution of the nursery and Headstart, most children participate in some preschool program too. After the fourth grade, the children go to the Clewiston public schools.

At the time of her first menses a girl used to be isolated in a special chickee. She ate alone and was not allowed salt for four days. Each evening as the evening star arose, she took a bath and cooked and ate. During this time she was not supposed to comb her hair. A girl is no longer isolated, but she still is not supposed to eat with the men of her family while she is menstruating, and

*Children sitting on Chickee platform.*

she cannot eat deer meat during this time. A menstruating woman still must not cook for men, and it is considered dangerous for her to step on bear's tracks, or to come in contact with medicine bundles. If a woman lives in a house, she should not sleep in the same bed as her husband during her period, or if they live in a chickee, she should not sleep with him under the same mosquito net. One girl said, "I know the old beliefs are silly, but I do not eat at the table with my father during my period. It would upset him if he thought I did that, and I respect him."

Boys no longer have an initiation ceremony at Big Cypress. It is said that any family wishing to have a son initiated could take him to the Green Corn Dance performed by the Tamiami Trail Indians.

First marriage usually takes place in the late teens for both sexes, and a girl is supposed to be a virgin at the time of her first marriage. However, it is widely believed that there are no virgins among the older teenagers. Formerly, punishment for adultery, incest, and loss of virginity before marriage was meted out at the Green Corn Dance, but there is no punishment for any of these acts any more.

There are no age sets for either sex, and adulthood is the period from marriage to death. Burials and mortuary practices are now under the guidance of the local Southern Baptist Church. The missionary who lives at Hollywood comes to Big Cypress for some services, and there are Indian deacons who conduct many ceremonies. In the old days, after a death, the surviving spouse was washed in a pond by a member of his own sex. A woman had all her necklaces removed and her hair put into one braid. She was dressed in black clothes. A man's hair was not cut for four months. A woman might continue mourning for two to four years, but a man's period of mourning was much less. During the mourning period the bereaved were expected to behave very solemnly. Some people told me that chickees were abandoned after a death. Others disagreed. On the fourth day after the death the body was placed in the woods and covered with logs, personal belongings were broken and buried with the body, and a fire was kept going at the head of the grave for four days and nights. These mortuary practices have not been observed for several decades. Burial is now in a small cemetery on the reservation, but some of the old people continue to observe weakened forms of the mourning ritual. At one time a widow or widower was expected to seek a new spouse in the clan of the deceased, but there is no longer any such expectation.

## Kinship Terminology

The old kinship terminology is disappearing. Many young people do not know or do not use the Indian terms for cousins, aunts, and uncles. Some of those in their twenties are frequently unable to recall all of the Mikasuki words for kinfolk. English kinship terms have become common with all but the older people, even though English is not spoken by many Indians. Some parents were quite astonished when they discovered that their children had never learned all the Indian kinship terms. At one time all the women of the father's clan were

*Aged woman.*

called the same term as that applied to the paternal and maternal grandmothers, but only the old people remember this. A typical system of Crow kinship terminology is thus changing into something akin to the Eskimo type. Even the maternal and paternal uncles are now often called by the English term. The merging of the uncles is doubtless in recognition of the change in authority structure. The mother and father, not the mother's brother, exercise what control there is over their children now.

Cousins and more distant relatives are both referred to and addressed by name, or just called "kinfolk." The changeover from the use of kin terms to personal names parallels the changes from traditional kinship relationships to behavior toward people on an individualistic basis.

Even incest prohibitions show this trend. Father's brother's children used to be called by the term applied to an older or younger sibling, and like a sibling they fell under the incest prohibition. Now they are referred to and addressed by their personal names or called the English "cousin." Some older people reported that at one time mother's brother's children could not be considered possible mates. There was disagreement about cousin marriages though, some people saying no cousin marriage was allowed, some saying that cross-cousin marriage was acceptable, and others contending that any cousin not in Ego's clan was a possible spouse. The application of the English term, cousin, is a response to the merging of those kinfolk as a change in behavior expectations occurred. Lately there have been three cousin marriages, and as in the case of broken clan exogamy, no one does anything about it except gossip a bit. The social and economic importance of kinship beyond the family has lessened and the terminology has changed to reflect the new role expectations. Most behavior is individualistic; in some cases personal names have been substituted for kin terms; and previously isolating terms have been merged in other cases.

# 6

# Political Organization

## History

THE CREEK OF GEORGIA AND ALABAMA had two categories of political organization, civil councils and war leaders. These categories are common to many of the southeastern Indians (Swanton 1946:*passim*). Councils were "white" categories concerned with the government of peace. War was the "red" category concerned with unfriendly intertribal relations. The peace chief was the civil head of his town and its highest ranking official. As explained above, the position of chief was hereditary within certain clans, but these clans varied from town to town and from time to time. The civil chief was assisted by a council and by another group called "beloved men" who were retired warriors. Driver (1961:346) has decribed three classes of warriors who had political authority:

> Their statuses were wholly achieved by valorous deeds of war. The highest class served as town police, punishing those who acted contrary to the will of the council or failed to attend the harvest ceremony. The intermediate class were less distinguished in war, but far enough along to have a voice in the council. The lowest warrior class included anyone who had killed an enemy and had brought back a scalp to prove it.

There was a war leader chosen by the warriors from the highest class. He was also a member of the council and acted as leader in time of war. Driver (1961: 347) continues:

> While we are not always told so, it seems certain that every officer, including the "peace" ones, got his start up the ladder of fame as a warrior. Once he had attained one of the more modest civil offices, he could progress to higher ones on the basis of oratorical ability, knowledge of tribal lore and law, administrative ability, and other such civil qualifications. It also seems likely that every officer could be impeached by the council.

The political picture is hazy for the Lower Creek, the Hitchiti speakers, for there is inadequate information. The civil chief could apparently come from more than one clan within the same community, and the clans of the chiefs also varied from town to town. During the period of stress when the three Seminole wars were being fought, general rules no longer could be applied because of the extinction of some clans or the lack of suitable candidates for office among those still living together. The war chiefs were not traditionally connected with any particular clan, but were chosen on the basis of ability. Therefore, it is not unexpected that there is no discoverable pattern of selecting leaders during the first part of this century at Big Cypress.

The early writers give totally inadequate information about the political situation. In 1875 an article in a popular magazine mentions a Seminole man called a subchief and also refers to the man's son-in-law as occupying that same role (Ober 1875:143). The author does not, however, say what activities are involved in the role subchief, and no informant at Big Cypress remembered any position with that title. Several writers (Ober 1875:144; Potter 1836:10, 30; MacCauley 1884:508) also refer to a chief called Tustenuggu by name. The word "Tustenug-gee," according to Swanton and others, is a title, although it appears to have been used as a name by the Florida Indians. Nevertheless, the aforementioned article tells no more about this man except to say that he had been elected chief instead of Tiger-Tail.

> After the ceremonies was (sic) over, they elected old Tustenuggu, chief, instead of Tiger-Tail, who had been chief so long, and that came near making a fight; but it was proved that Tustenuggu was descended from old Micanopy, and ought to have been chief long ago (Ober 1875:144).

Micanopy was from the Snake clan, which is extinct at Big Cypress now.

MacCauley (1884:508–509) gives a brief description of the political organization as it appeared to him in 1880:

> There is, however, among these Indians a simple form of government, to which the inhabitants of at least the three southern settlements submit. . . .
>
> So far as there is a common seat of government, it is located at Fish Eating Creek, where reside the head chief and big medicine man of the Seminole, Tus-ta-nug-ge, and his brother, hos-pa-ta-ki, also a medicine man. These two are called the Tus-ta-nug-ul-ki, or "great heroes" of the tribe. At this settlement, annually, a council composed of minor chiefs from the various settlements, meets and passes upon the affairs of the tribe.
>
> What the official organization of the tribe is I do not know.

MacCauley was told that there were two war chiefs, two little chiefs, and one medicine man at Big Cypress, but he does not divulge their names, their functions, nor the extent of their authority.

Lucien A. Spencer, Seminole Agent, said in the Annual Report of 1913:

> The business of the tribe is transacted by a Council composed of the Head Men of the various clans. The Florida Seminoles have no chief, but the oldest man of each clan is Patriarch or Head Man of that clan, and these Head Men form a council which is absolute control (sic) of all affairs of the tribe (Seminole Indian Agency 1913:13).

This council organization is probably the same as the one Nash (1931:26) referred to:

This tribal council decrees penalties for infractions of their code, and in years past undoubtedly has inflicted the death penalty. Spencer says it takes cognizance of marriage and divorce, although certainly much marriage and divorce take no cognizance of it.

Questions were asked to determine who were leaders in the years between the Nash report of 1930, and the tribal reorganization of 1957. Frequently the response was that there were no real leaders, but when men were named, the choice was based on the fact that the men selected spoke English or that they had been instrumental in furthering good Indian-white relations. Four people said that the leaders of that period were the trustees who were Indian appointees of the Commissioner of Indian Affairs. Five people named a *white* man as leader because he could speak "Indian" and because he had tried to help the Indians. Of the three most frequently named leaders from the decade before reorganization, two were elected to the council and board after the tribe was reorganized under the Wheeler-Howard Act. The third was an elderly medicine man, who, Sturtevant (1960:522) said, ". . . has more white friends and acquaintances than any other Seminole his age, and he is much more responsive and unreserved in meeting white people than any other Seminole I know."

The only common qualities discernible among the men named as leaders during that time period are the ability to speak both English and "Indian" (and sometimes both Mikasuki and Muskogee), and a willingness to act as intermediary between the white world and the reservation. A former council representative from Big Cypress is the son of one of the members of the council during Nash's time, but in a matrilineal society, positions are not passed from father to son, and his election to office was the result of factors other than kinship. No one was reported to be a leader either because of his ritual status or his clan membership.

The younger people, who understand better what "leader" means in contemporary American political terms, denied there were any real leaders. As one of these younger people put it:

> Before the tribe was organized, there were no real leaders in the way you mean. There were older men who talked together and then when everyone agreed, they decided what to do. Sometimes white men would go to one Indian because he could speak English and then that Indian would talk to the tribe and explain what the white men wanted. Sometimes white men thought that this man was a leader, but there was no leader, just all the people who were living all over. Josie Billie says he was a leader, he even said he was a chief, but the people never thought he was a chief. He did cures, but not everyone went to him for cures even. He liked to be a big man, but he really wasn't. Johnny Cypress helped get roads, but he was not a real leader either. If other people did not agree with him, he couldn't make them do what he say. A long time ago there were leaders, but when I was little there weren't any.

Younger people such as this informant very clearly conceive of leadership only when there is some sort of coercive power.

## The Seminole Tribe of Florida—the Polity

The Indian Reorganization Act of 1934 allowed groups of Indians to incorporate and form a body politic with elected officials to manage tribal affairs.

A federal constitution, ratified in August, 1957, organized the Seminole Tribe of Florida in which membership was restricted to those who made formal application and were of Seminole blood. The constitution and by-laws provided for membership of people of one quarter or more degree of Seminole Indian blood through written application to the tribal council and the majority approval of the council. In 1963 the total enrollment was 862 out of approxiamtely 1200 Indians in Florida. Today members live not only on the three reservations under tribal jurisdiction, but also in Miami, Ft. Pierce, Immokalee, and along the Tamiami Trail.

The territorial jurisdiction of the Seminole Tribe of Florida includes the reservations of Hollywood, Brighton, and Big Cypress, lands held under Executive Order 1379 of 1911, and any other land which may be acquired for the use and benefit of the tribe. The Florida state reservation land is under the joint administration of the Seminole Tribe of Florida and the Miccosukee Tribe, which is under a separate agency. Although there are kinship ties between the members of the Seminole Tribe of Florida and some members of the Miccosukee Tribe, the latter has no political connection with the former and will not come under further consideration.

Big Cypress supplied three members to the committee which cooperated with the Bureau of Indian Affairs in drawing up the constitution. The constitution was ratified by a vote of 241 to 5 with 55 percent of the eligible voters casting ballots.

The reorganization gave the Indians the opportunity to govern themselves subject to federal guardianship in certain spheres. Under the constitution of the tribe, an elected five member council became the governing body replacing any previous political system. The members of the council are elected by secret ballot and majority vote.

The five members constituting the tribal council are a chairman elected at-large, three councilmen elected from and exclusively by the residents of the three reservations, and the president of the board of directors (see below) who serves as vice-chairman during his term of office. The constitution also provides for the selection of committees and a secretary-treasurer to the council. Committeemen are selected for a period of two years or until the next election of councilmen. Any person twenty-one years or older who has lived on one of the reservations for four continuous years immediately prior to candidacy and who is a member of the tribe is eligible to be a candidate for election to the council. Members who are not residents of any reservation vote only for at-large candidates. Resident voters select the representative of their own reservation plus the at-large candidates. To become a candidate any qualified member of the Seminole Tribe of Florida must have a petition signed by ten eligible voters from his or her reservation, or, for an at-large candidate, by ten voters from each reservation. The signers must not have signed petitions for any other candidate in that election.

The tribal council is empowered to negotiate with federal, state, and local governments, to employ legal counsel for the tribe, to manage tribal lands, to confer with the Secretary of the Interior on behalf of the tribe, and to make and enforce certain ordinances, to adopt resolutions, and to function as an advisory and governing body in the manner set out in the constitution.

Before the Seminole Tribe of Florida was organized, the Indians lived according to traditional law. For breaches of conduct within the reservation borders, only such social control as deemed necessary by other Indians was brought to bear on the offender. Since their organization, the council has passed a resolution giving the state and county civil and criminal jurisdiction over the three reservations. This resolution became a law by act of the legislature of the state of Florida July 1, 1961. From time to time, Indians have been deputized. However, in practice, the state authority does not extend to purely internal social control unless some well-known law is broken. Even then Indians are reluctant to bring in state police, and any one doing so is made to feel like an informer. Therefore, state authorities are usually called in only when a white person is involved or when there is a very serious offense.

## The Seminole Tribe of Florida, Inc.—the Corporation

The Seminole organization is unique in the dual nature of its governmental structure. It is divided into the political arm, the council-governed Seminole Tribe of Florida, and the business organization, the Seminole Tribe of Florida, Incorporated, a federally chartered corporation governed by a board of directors. This separation of power is uncommon among Indian groups reorganized under the Wheeler-Howard Act of 1934. Because these two organizational bodies are so similarly named, the political body will hereafter be referred to simply as the tribe, and the business organization will be called the corporation.

The corporation was organized in 1957 at the same time as, but separate from, the tribe. The corporation has the responsibility for the development and management of the tribal resources. It is the business organization of the tribe with an executive body of five directors, one elected from each reservation; one at-large, who is the president, and a vice-president, who is the chairman of the tribal council. The purpose of the corporation is stated in the amended corporate charter Article II, Section 1:

> . . . to further the economic development of the Seminole Tribe of Florida by conferring upon said tribe certain corporate rights, powers, privileges, and immunities; to secure for the members of the tribe an assured economic independence; and to provide for the proper exercise by the tribe of various functions heretofore performed by the Department of the Interior. . . .

All persons who are members of the Seminole Tribe of Florida are also shareholders in the Seminole Tribe of Florida, Inc. Shareholders' meetings may be called by the board of directors or by a petition of not less than 20 percent of the voting shareholders. Questions may be voted on by the membership at these meetings, but since there have been only two since 1957, most of the decisions are made by the board of directors using their authority as executive managers of the corporation. The economic authority of the board is circumscribed by the need for authorization by the Secretary of the Interior in such matters as sales of land or mineral rights. The corporation may borrow funds to use for productive enterprises or to lend to the shareholders from the Indian credit fund or elsewhere. The Indian credit fund was established by the federal government to give financial help to Indian groups incorporated under the Indian Reorganization Act of 1934.

The corporation numbers among its accomplishments the creation of the Seminole Arts and Crafts Center and the Seminole Okalee Indian Village enterprise, both of which are located at the Hollywood Reservation on the coast, where they constitute a major Seminole tourist attraction. Indian people are employed in sales and as guides through the village which purports to show tourists the history and customs of the Seminole. The employees are Hollywood residents, for Big Cypress and Brighton are too far away for commuting.

Another important creation of the corporation is the Seminole Indian Land Development Enterprise. It is through this enterprise that the land at Brighton and Big Cypress is being developed into improved pasturage for the cattle program. The land development is financed through grazing fees paid by cattle owners at the reservations and through funds made available by the Indian revolving loan program. The branch of land operations of the agency and the state extension service offer technical assistance. The corporation also provides low interest loans to eligible members of the tribe. These loans include short-term, house, cattle, and small business loans.

## Control by the Agency

The constitution and charter give the tribe a well-defined political structure with representation from all three reservations to decide on matters of importance. However, there is no sphere from which the Bureau of Indian Affairs or its local representatives are absolutely barred.

Probably the most powerful form of control the white man has over the Indian comes from agency control of funds for house and cattle loans, and the agency's control over the repayment of these loans. Any Indian receiving economic assistance from the United States government finds himself under agency supervision to a degree that does not exist among borrowers in the general population. The agency branch of credit must approve loans for houses, cattle, small business, and furthermore has the power to take money for repayment of principal and interest out of Indian cattle sales before an individual gets the check for the sale. This situation has frequently resulted in no cash income to the owner, a consequence many owners do not understand at all.

Corporately the tribal board of directors cannot borrow more than $10,000 from the Indian credit fund without the express approval of the Secretary of the Interior or his authorized representative. The charter specifies agency or Bureau of Indian Affairs control over the corporation. Amendments to the charter must be approved by the Secretary of the Interior. Indeed, the Secretary of the Interior had to approve the charter, the constitution, and the by-laws before they were offered to the tribe for ratification. The requirement that the chairman of the council and the president of the board must leave their home reservations and move to the headquarters reservation at Hollywood for their terms of office is seen by some Indians as serving to place them under the closer scrutiny, if not control, of the agency officials.

The council can employ lawyers for the protection of tribal rights, but the choice of attorney and his fee must be approved by the Secretary of the Interior, and annual budget requests are subject to his approval also. Books and records of the treasurer must be audited at least once every year, or anytime the Commissioner of Indian Affairs feels such action is advisable. Copies of the audit must be sent to the superintendent, the area director, and the commissioner. However, all officers and employees of the Department of the Interior as well as the Indians are bound by the provisions of the charter, constitutions, and by-laws. Many Indians, unfamiliar with legal documents, do not realize that contracts are binding on all signing parties, and that the Indians are protected as well as circumscribed by these legalities. As John Collier, Commissioner of Indian Affairs at the time the Indian Reorganization Act was passed, has said,

> Over Indian matters . . . Congress still holds plenary power. But in the Indian Reorganization Act, and in some other related Indian statutes, Congress through general legislation has adopted self-restraining ordinances. The Reorganization Act furnishes a flexible system for the devolution of authority from the government . . . to the tribes. . . . It is true that . . . these acts explicitly or by implication affirm that federal responsibility continue, no matter how far the devolution shall go (Collier 1947:168–169).

In addition to the controls specified in the corporate charter and the constitution, members of the agency staff or associated bodies have considerable control over the Seminole through superior technical knowledge. The lack of education or even familiarity with day-to-day business affairs puts rather severe limits on choice by many Indians. Few Indians have the information necessary to make intelligent selections among the types of loans they may apply for, and individuals may not take loans for unspecified purposes. They do not understand interest and principal. They have had no experience with the concept of percentage. Consequently they simply do what they are told when they go to the agency to apply for funds. If they plan to put in a well and a pump, the loan money is applied directly to that purpose, not given to individuals to pay bills as they are incurred. It is very difficult for most Indians to borrow money in the general money market. A few of them who have paid off government cattle loans have been able to borrow from private sources such as banks in order to increase their herds after available government money was used up. But most Indians do not have this source of funds, for Indians are not considered good financial risks, and so they must go to the agency or not borrow money.

Another type of control through technical competence lies in the fact that an agency representative attends all meetings: council, board, and cattlemen's association. The agency man knows the rules of procedure of formal meetings, the writing of minutes, ordinances, resolutions, motions, proper voting methods, etc., and is in a position to control the meetings if need be. The Indians have resented the fact that a government man is always present, but there is nothing they can do about it. A complaint about this was brought up at the board meeting once. The Indians were disturbed about the superintendent and the administrative officer attending a meeting of the cattle association. The Indians claimed that the agency people did not have any connection with the cattle association. The superintendent replied that this was not true because the association was operating with government funds and the agency men were there to advise on all operations of the tribe. The stand was unanswerable. The Indians did not know whether the superintendent was right or wrong, but they could not debate with him because they could not quote rules and regulations the way the government people did. This is an example of very effective control by government personnel. Unless the Indians appeal to other, non-agency white people—which they are reluctant to do—they have no one to advise them except these agency people. To date there have been no Indians with enough education to meet the agency men on their own ground. The government employees look upon the supervision as necessary to prevent financial disaster until there are better trained Indians, and to protect the interests of the vast majority of Indians from more aggressive, self-interested individuals who might take advantage of the ignorance of the rest of the people.

The jobs which are open to the Indians in the Bureau itself are the best paying employment that Indians have. At Big Cypress there are three federal employees working on the road program, one working on land development, and another working in the capacity of caretaker-janitor at the school and health clinic. The incomes of the five men are among the highest on the reservation. The workers have to conform to the work standards of the federal government to obtain and keep these jobs. There is therefore control exerted upon these people through pressures to conform in order to keep the jobs. Other Indians have been employed by the government at times, but generally they have not proven satisfactory, and those who could not meet the demands of the agency have lost their employment. The five men who are currently employed by the Bureau of Indian Affairs are well respected by their employers. The supervisor of the federal road-building program said:

> I find them in every way the equivalent of heavy equipment operators in the general population. They are prompt, skillful, and put in a full day's work. They have never stayed off the job without asking permission first or letting me know in case of sickness. They make $2.83 per hour as road equipment operators. That is very good pay for these people, and it is the same per hour pay that people of the same skill get in Florida road work. It may even be a little higher in some cases.

All the men employed by the government care about keeping their jobs. Under most circumstances, therefore, Indian employees will conform to the expectations of the employer. Even men who work for the tribe, not the government, come under the power of the agency more than may appear on the surface. Though the tribe pays the salaries, there is no member of the council or board capable of directing the work, so it is the land operations officer of the agency who is the *de facto* supervisor. Technically, employees of the tribe are free to decide on matters in the field, but actually they always wait until the appropriate government official comes to the reservation to inspect the work. This is typical of the dependence the Indian employees have on direction from the agency. They are unwilling to take the responsibility for decisions in which they are uncertain of their competence.

Effecive authority stems from the agency personnel who through control of finances and superior technical know-how can see to it that the men they want are the men who are hired. Everyone on the tribal payroll knows he must please the agency as well as the tribe. Employees do not have necessary experience and must do what the agency officials think should be done. Many different kinds of resources can be used in the control of decision-making: money and credit, job control, information control, knowledge and expertise, and legality, among others. All these factors may be seen at work in the instances given above.

The federal government exerts pressure in smaller ways too, pressure which is often very irritating to the Indians. The health officer forced one man to stop selling certain unpackaged foods because of poor sanitary conditions, and at the powwow, a county sanitarian under contract to the Bureau of Indian Affairs must supervise food preparation and sanitation. Even the powwow contests are directed by white people from the agency. In 1964 and 1965 there was not a single Indian on any of the judging committees. Some Indians resent this as unnecessary interference, even in the case of maintenace of sanitary controls, for they do not understand the dangers of food poisoning.

The government has expended very little effort to justify its stand in this respect. Lines of communication run through the elected officials, and the officials do not always explain the ways of the agency to the people. Even a service such as periodic inspections of dwellings and spraying for vermin is not well received because it is not understood, and it is often badly timed, for example, coming without notice when the women are too occupied to have their homes upset with spraying.

## Leadership and Authority

The leadership is most effective in dealing with external problems. The representatives are acceptable primarily in terms of external struggle, dealing with the agency or with other sectors of outside society. Internally there is no one who appears to be considered a genuine leader, nor is there any group of people such as clan elders who jointly may be considered constituting internal leadership.

Within the group the role of leader is weak, not backed up with any means of enforcement. Leadership is informal and persuasive. Most people are not willing to give leaders a wide range of responsibility and authority. The only power the leaders have is found in some sort of collective support, and most decisions are still collective decisions. The emerging leadership at Big Cypress still does not have enough self-confidence to try decision-making without manifest support in matters deemed important. Since there is no group of economically, socially, or politically prominent people except for the leadership itself, there is no part of the population with enough power or authority to give the leaders the strength to ignore the wishes of the "lower people."

The constitution and by-laws legitimize the power of the elected officials but they provide no means of enforcement. Enforcement exists only through moral persuasion or economic threat. There is no provision for police action except in cases where the state or county has jurisdiction. The power of the decision-makers lies primarily in their roles as mediators between the reservation and the outside world, because the inhabitants prefer using their elected officials as emissaries to the rest of the world. If the leaders were to refuse such service, the inhabitants would have to make outside contact themselves and they do not wish to do that. The members of the outside society, in their turn, also achieve contact with Big Cypress people almost entirely through the persons of the leaders. The leaders thus have the power by default. No one else wants their job. Most people shun political responsibility. The statements are many and forceful that they do not want to tell other people what to do. Two typical exerpts from interviews on this subject follow.

> I guess it's not pleasant to be an officer. Some people are always getting mad at you, they get on your back. People talk about you. Even when you try to help, some people think you are wrong. I wouldn't want the job, and I wouldn't want my wife to be on the board or council. It's a hard thing. We need good elected officials, but there aren't many good people who will take the job. Our present representatives are about the only ones, seems like.

> I would not run for office. Never, never. Everyone blames you if things go wrong even if you try to do right. I don't like people mad at me. I would not like to run for office and be treated like that. There are some people you can work with, but most of them you can't. I'll just try to take care of my family and keep them out of trouble.

During all my time at Big Cypress, only two men said that they had been thinking about running for office. One of those men did eventually run and was elected. He resigned from office long before his term was out.

Group identity and group security are still seen in terms of unanimity at Big Cypress. Maintaining this identity and security is basic to the way in which the leadership role is played. Any real attempt to override the will of the people results in so much grumbling and critical innuendo that the leaders' self-confidence is destroyed. Votes in the council or board are not taken until the leaders are already almost certain of the outcome. One representative said on this subject,

> We never vote when anyone is mad. We just talk and talk until everyone understands. If some people are still mad, we don't vote then. We put it off until another meeting. If we have to get something changed which people don't like or don't understand, we may have to talk for a very long time, but it is best for everyone to agree before we vote.

Tribal administration has not yet reached the point where people become merely parts of a formal organization. The Big Cypress people prefer the collective security in which the group as a whole is more important than any individual. Therefore, one of the frequently heard grievances is that expressed against individuals who are thought to be getting preferred treatment of any sort. The charges most often leveled at the leadership are accusations of authoritarianism, special treatment, or individualism.

When the collective action begins to break down as it must under representative government and the need for rapid action on issues, the main means of curtailing individual aggression begins to break down. At Big Cypress individual aggression has been expressed in vandalism at the recreation hall, and in such senseless destruction as smashed floodlights at the health clinic and school, an arson attempt at the Big Cypress Post Office, and petty thievery, unknown until recently. Bewilderment about the political situation was expressed by one informant,

> It isn't good to tell people what to do. Someone gets mad. I wouldn't like to have people mad at me. The people at the agency want us to do some things we never used to do, and the leaders are supposed to tell people to do it. Then no one likes the leaders. Most people wouldn't like to be a leader. I wouldn't like to be a leader. I think it is good to wait until everyone agrees, but sometimes they say we can't wait until everyone agrees because we have to do something right away. We don't like that.

The fieldwork at Big Cypress indicated that there is at least an unformulated belief that leaders who govern best, govern least. The Indians do not like to be told what to do either by white men or by their own people. On the other hand, the community never initiates action. How then do things get done? Is it a matter largely left to chance or to long term wearing away of community inertia and opposition? Since the decision-makers feel they must persuade the citizenry before a decision is made, they procrastinate to let people become accustomed to the new idea or situation behind the decision. The agency people always see speed as the important factor, but they overlook the damage that speed might do to psychic as well as to economic, political, and social structures. There is always the possibility that the result will be alienation of individuals from both cultures, Indian and general Floridian. Although there are differences of opinion about whether public interest is better served by speed through a majority vote or by unanimity, there is no doubt that the latter is much slower. The agency people would like to see decisions made rapidly on the basis of majority vote.

Majority vote often seems capricious to the Indian people, and the leaders do not want to appear capricious and thereby subject themselves to criticism from the people. They want their decisions to be accepted as judicious and obviously the best possible. Since equality is so important at Big Cypress, and since there is very little social distance between the leaders and the rest of the community, the decision-makers do not want to have to force unpopular decisions on their constitutents, even though they have authority by virtue of having been elected. They still consider themselves one of the crowd, and there is no evidence of any cult of personality or charisma. By the vote power rests formally upon the entire community, which has the tradition of unanimity. Since there are no organizations or factions with subleaders, decision-makers are relieved of any necessity of developing policies to appeal to segments of the population or to reward or bribe heads of factions. The opposition takes an unstructured form, general passive resistance. Therefore, the decision-makers must seek approval anew for each controversial decision. This is truly "consent of the governed," for in a sense the decision-makers are polling the constituents on every issue.

The agency exerts influence on the elected officials that is pointed and structured dealing as it does with specific technological or financial issues. Pressure on the officials from the Big Cypress inhabitants is diffuse and unstructured. Voting laws and pressure from the agency level come into conflict with the custom of unanimity and negative evaluation of personal pressures from the community level. The outside society tries to exert pressure in the desired direction to bring about agreement and change, whereas the Indian leaders prefer to achieve the same result by diminishing antagonistic elements among their constituents. The decision-makers think that this is the best way to a solution. It is less stressful, but it takes longer. The leaders want to diminish opposition before decision, but agency people want a decision, and then pressure on the people to accept it. As one leader says, "I go talk to the people and tell them about things. Then I go away and let them think it over. If it seems like they are mad, I go back and talk some more. I don't argue."

The result is that two concepts of leadership meet in the role of the Indian decision-makers. The agency feels that as leaders they should "lead," that is, initiate action, make decisions, and see that these decisions are implemented. The Indians see leaders as spokesmen who explain their needs to the agency. Leaders by Indian definition of leadership are ineffective in Western eyes. Leaders conforming to the Western model would be "bossy" in the eyes of the Indians, who are not accustomed to accepting hierarchical authority and would probably resent it strongly enough to get rid of any leader who acted in such a way.

Since leaders must be acceptable to both Indians and the agency, the extreme choices of either would not be tolerable. Compromise is important. The ideal representative according to Indian opinion is a man who helps the people; who does not become inflated with his own self-importance; and who can deal successfully with members of the dominant society. The ideal representative by white standards is a man who will initiate and direct action; who will meet hour and labor standards of the general society; who is preferably not too "Indian" or strange; and who has the backing of his people. Therefore the men who are elected and remain in office must be sensitive to both concepts and capable of considerable versatility.

## Rewards of Leadership

It is difficult to determine the rewards sought by the decision-makers, for tangible rewards such as money, goods, and land do not accrue. The leaders are in the upper income brackets on the reservation, but they were there prior to, not because of, their election. Doubtless they see elective office as a means of protecting what they have, but there appears to be another form of reward which keeps the officials in office. That reward is, I believe, satisfaction in doing a necessary job which no one else wants. Certainly there is no prestige or honor connected with an elective position. If there is any prestige, it comes not from the Indian people, but from the outside society where election to public office is considered something of an honor. As far as the Indians go, entering an election does not make one a "big man"—even if one wins. Should he lose, it results in something very like loss of face, and candidates who would accept nomination to run are hard to find. No one wants to lose, but very few men want to win either because the office brings burdens in excess of rewards. It does appear, then, that rewards must come almost entirely in the form of personal satisfaction, as expressed here:

> If people elect me, they must be willing to let me decide for them, and they must believe that I will try to do the very best thing I can do. Somebody has to be a leader even if it is hard and sometimes people get mad. I think it is a good thing to help all the people.

Two leaders during my stays on the reservation did report that they were rewarded by the idea of helping their people. The leadership position gives a decision-maker the opportunity to do civic service in his community and to achieve a status position which is meaningful in the dominant society. Thus, the leaders can, on the face of it, probably achieve an image of self that is more gratifying than that image would be if they remained apathetic to community problems. Concepts from the outside society have seeped in, and the leaders are more responsive to these external values than most of the other Indians. Two representatives have made statements which show their awareness of these concepts:

> If they elect someone, they have to let that person do what he thinks is right. Sometimes the leaders are in a position to learn more than the others. If the people don't think the leaders are doing right, they have to vote for more leaders. That is the way it is when you vote.

> I try to set an example like when something is voted on and maybe I thought it should be some other way, after a majority votes, I do it the way it was voted.

There may be other reasons for holding office. Public office is exciting, and the old way of life may seem obscure and boring by comparison. The leaders sometimes take trips to Washington, Tallahassee, and Gainesville, where the state university is located. Activities of the officials are perhaps simply more stimulting and challenging. It is difficult to measure an appeal of this sort.

## Indian People and the Agency

From what has already been said about the reluctance of the people to deal directly with the agency, it will be concluded that they regard the agency with suspicion and mistrust. Most Indians refuse to communicate with the agency beyond a bare minimum. They consider the Bureau of Indian Affairs and its local representatives unpredictable and authoritarian. There is a frequent complaint that the federal government does not understand the Indians' problems and really does not care. Sometimes they say that perhaps government is not really necessary. Government and bureaucracy are thus reified by the Indians, many of whom like and respect individuals who work for the local agency. The individual Indian is, consequently, glad to let the leaders make most of the contacts with the agency.

One situation calling for contact between individuals and agency personnel is the need for a personal loan. An Indian with this problem will go to Hollywood with an interpreter, usually a young relative, to arrange to borrow money or to refinance a loan. This is done without any assistance from the leaders. In fact, this type of situation is usually kept private, just between the credit officer and the individual. The elected leaders do not enter into the picture unless for some reason the individual case is taken up at a meeting of the board of directors. Borrowers often complain, not about interest rates or any financial problems, but rather because "They talk so loud" at the agency, or "They make me wait so long." Vague accusations of this nature are rationalized explanations to disguise the deep discomfort and general suspicion the Indians feel about having to sign or make their marks and thumb prints on legal papers and about other puzzles in the world of finance. Some mysterious "they" seem to make all the decisions, and the perplexed individual may come to suspect that selfish interests are being served. The leaders do not play a role in these situations. But in other situations, the leaders are the means of buffering external pressure on the community in an impersonal way. Indeed, they actually serve to keep the pressures from becoming personal.

Some workers at the agency know a number of Big Cypress residents by sight, but no one can recognize and name all the adults on the reservation. Most agency people do not visit the reservation very often, and they often make statements about the reservation which seem to indicate little familiarity with the conditions there. They keep innumerable records on individuals, but they do not have much first-hand contact with them and their way of life. There is no social interaction, only general supervision and record keeping.

The residents of Big Cypress respond to agency people passively. It is a form of protective coloration since the Indians are never quite sure what to expect from agency employees. The Indians do not know how to act except not to act at all. By refusing to talk, by speaking in monosyllables, or by pretending not to understand any English, the Indians soon frustrates efforts at conversation, and the uncomfortable white person, used to small-talk, soon leaves the Indian alone.

## Personal Characteristics of the Leaders

The men who have held office have not had much in common. Some have been long-time residents of Big Cypress; some are recent arrivals. Clan membership has varied. Two of the elected officials have been divorced in state courts. One divorce met with widespread approval; the other one was greatly disapproved. A number of people believe that the second divorce was an important factor in the defeat of the man when he next ran for election.

Until the late sixties, elected officials were mature men, but in recent years more young people, including women, have run for office. Two young men have been elected. Although there is some belief that younger people should be active in reservation affairs and should be training for future work, most adults are wary of youthful rashness and folly. The men in their twenties who were elected have not held office more than one term, and one of those men resigned after only a few months in office. His short tenure was the result of his disaffection in a role where he exercised very little power and often had very little public support. Lack of public support from men privately pledged to his goals angered one official who made the following statement at a general meeting:

> You say to me when we are alone that you do not like the way things are run and you think I should do something about it. Now when the time has come to speak up, you remain silent. I have tried to help you, but now you let me down.

The private life of the man just quoted was such that he was soundly beaten the next time he ran for office. He has lived off the reservation for most of the past decade. Many of the cattle owners respect his ability as a cattleman, for he has worked with cattle for a long time both on and off the reservation. He considers himself a sort of opposition leader, and he looks toward the future when he hopes he will again hold office. No one else gives him much chance for a comeback. Discussing his political outlook, he said,

> We need younger people in office. Educated people, English speaking. Many people come to me for advice. They look to me to tell them what to do. The present leaders don't go to the people and explain things to them. They just tell them what they think the people should know. That is usually just what the white men want them to know. A good leader should explain things to the people so they really understand. The white people never go to the Indians, just to the leaders. I would go to the people. I take their side.

Nevertheless, the people rejected him.

Elected officials are now becoming visibly different from most of the other inhabitants at Big Cypress, a trend which may be the result and indication of incipient social stratification. They own homes which are kept in better condition than many others, lawns are cut, woodwork is painted regularly. Their cars are newer and cleaner. Their clothes are more fashionable and are kept in better condition. They keep their appliances in good working condition too, rather than allowing them to deteriorate to the point of uselessness. In 1965 the family owning the most equipment showed a surprising array: an outboard motor boat and boat trailer, the only color television set at Big Cypress, a black and white television set, three electric fans, a vacuum cleaner, a station wagon, two transistor radios, washing machine, two sewing machines, two refrigerators, an adding machine, ironing board and iron, and three foam-rubber Hollywood type beds, a live parakeet and a cage, a wide assortment of contemporary children's toys, as well as the necessary furniture for bed, dining, and living rooms.

A brief sketch of one man who has won whenever he has run for office will offer an example of a successful and respected leader. He is often mentioned as a man who tries to help the people, a civic virtue greatly admired by Mikasuki. Every election which he has entered he has won by a substantial margin (44 to 8 in 1965). He is one of the major cattle owners and is employed by the tribe on the land development program. Not only is he considered a good worker by the tribal officers, he is also highly regarded and consulted by the white government employees. His salary is one of the highest at Big Cypress. On the questionnaire administered to the cattle owners, he was designated as a leader, and in interviews with the noncattle owning residents, he was named as an important man. The personnel at the agency call him a leader and reinforce this role by seeking him out to act as intermediary for them. County and state officials use him in the same capacity whenever they must contact people on the reservation about matters arising from health, legal, or business problems. For their part, the other Indians have often taken their contact problems to him to get his assistance as go-between or arbitrator.

This elected representative is a middle-aged man with several grandchildren. He has no formal education and speaks only a little English. He does, however, understand English much better than he speaks it, and he has taught himself to read whatever is pertinent to his work. Perhaps more important than his self-education is his success in emulating the wage earners in the general population. He exhibits the approved middle-class virtues of punctuality, perseverance, and reliability, the lack of which has caused so many other Indians to lose jobs and political positions. These attributes have led to successful salaried jobs and a career as political representative of Big Cypress. At one time, this official worked for the Bureau of Indian Affairs, but when the tribe needed a man to supervise land development, he took that job even though it paid less. His stated reason for the change was his desire to make people in the tribe begin to think and act in terms of community, not for themselves or their families.

> We have not been used to living as a group of people. We grew up scattered about with each man taking care of his own family. Now it is different. We all live close together and we must all get together to help. If Big Cypress is going to be a good place to live we have to do this, otherwise the people who want to have a good life for their children will leave, and only old people and lazy people will be left. If we are going to have something worth while, we will all have to make it that way and stop just thinking about ourselves. So I decided I could help by seeing that the land was developed right—because I knew that the state extension agent knew what to do and we didn't. But some people would not have done what he said, so I took the job so it would be done right.

His actions should not be interpreted as pure altruism. He owns one of the largest cattle herds, and he knows that for the good of his cattle, he must have the fine pastures and veterinary care recommended by the extension service. He also knows that he cannot have those things alone but only as a part of the total cattle and land development program, which to be successful must be participated in by all the cattle owners. Still, he has greater vision than most of the other adult Indians. He understands the need for community action and the necessary technological requirements and he perceives that if potential leadership leaves the reservation, the people left will never be able to make the change to modern economic life. In other words, he seems to have a real feel for leadership and its benefits as well as a sense of responsibility toward his constituents.

## Political Attitudes

The Indian concept of proper democratic processes is a very low level of political dominance. Everyone should be left alone to do what he wants. Neighbor should not interfere with neighbor, and no one should tell anyone else what to do. Individualism and individual autonomy are the most important precepts. Democracy is not seen as entailing any sort of united effort to work toward community betterment or to make recalcitrant members behave according to approved standards.

Concommitant with the search for autonomy of the individual is the search for unanimity for any decisions which must be made for the community as a whole. The people do not like the concept of majority rule, for with a majority decision, a discontented minority results. The majority, by forcing the minority into acceptance, is thereby destroying the rights of some individuals. Majority decision is too final. The search for unanimity always allows further negotiation.

What effort there is at social control comes in the form of gossip. The Indians do not like to be talked about any more than they like people to interfere in more direct ways. The importance of equality and tolerance toward all other Big Cypress inhabitants is tempered with social control by means of gossip. If anyone starts acting the "big shot," the older men and women soon start gossiping about his behavior. While gossips have little effect on some of the younger people, the middle-aged and older definitely do not like to be talked about. In the absence of other means, gossip performs the function of social control. It is a way of letting people know that others do not approve their conduct without actually interfering with others' activities. The Indians are especially careful not to make unfavorable comments directly to a person, but the subject of the gossip always finds out somehow what is being said about him. If he is really perturbed, he will stop whatever activities the rest of the community disapprove. If he does not care, he will just ignore the gossip, secure in the knowledge that no one will actually do anything.

Aberrant behavior requires no explanation by the people. The freedom to be eccentric is guaranteed by the cultural tradition of individual autonomy. This tradition presents problems for the leaders because the general American society frowns on such deviance and expects the leaders to hold their people in line. Leaders are loath to interfere with personal idiosyncracies. Such idiosyncracies are not nearly so objectionable to the Indians as the individual who appears to place himself above the rest of the people, one who tries to break out of the framework of equality. "He thinks he is better than the rest of us," is just about the worst epithet that can be applied to a man.

These traits of individual autonomy, unanimity, control only by gossip, all stem from a deeply devout belief in human equality. No person or group is considered "better" than any other. People may excel at certain tasks, and some may have achieved a higher standard of living, but social equality is the basic quality in the value system at Big Cypress.

## Political Participation

The decision-makers must walk a tight rope between the all-out effort demanded by the agency and the stultifying slowness of the traditional Indian demand for unanimity before any action is carried out. The values and goals of all the residents at Big Cypress are not necessarily similar or even compatible.

At one extreme, the goals may be complete modernization; at the other, the smallest possible amount of change. The decision-makers must strive for some sort of congruence of aims. With disparate goals, effective group action is difficult, and the leaders must increase the amount of group information and win people over to a new point of view, or passive resistance and conflict result. Communication on technical matters, especially matters of finance, is difficult and takes time. Sometimes, however, instead of delay there is a push for rash action. The leaders must avoid these extremes and imbalances. Obviously political and psychological subtlety is required. Leaders must be careful not to commit the group to activities for which it has no skill, experience, or motivation, even though the agency may be pressing in that direction.

The people at Big Cypress have had no experience in organizing substructures to raise morale and the information level. Timing is very important in the decision-making situation. The right man must be at the right place when he is needed or important decisions may not be implemented from lack of direction or experience. There are no organized groups which could help the leaders. The Indians do not seek multiple membership in association groups even though the constitution and bylaws make provisions for various committees. Indians who have served on committees have not been happy with the results. They have usually felt that they were interfering with other people, and with the exception of a few teenagers who belong to 4-H clubs and the church membership, there are no voluntary associations at Big Cypress. Committees could be powerful in implementing decisions and could also serve as communication lines. Voluntary groups could be means of access to officialdom, but Big Cypress people do not see it that way. They look upon association as a form of snooping or coercion of individuals. The individual participates, if he participates at all, only as an individual, voting as means of personal participation in the political structure, and not as a member of any sort of pressure group or lobby. Or he expresses himself by not voting, either to protest or to show that he does not understand. The individual does not band together with other protesting or confused individuals to seek explanation or change.

One informant who was a teller for the first election in 1957, and has been a teller several times since, pointed out that there seems to be a smaller turnout at each election. Election records seem to bear out the contention, although all the voting figures are not available. If it is true, it may be inferred that the importance of each person who actually does vote has been increased in choosing the leaders. In the election of 1965, of the 16 people signing the winner's petition of candidacy, 15 actually voted. Of the 16 signing his opponent's petition, only 8 voted. In the 1957 election for the board, 117 people from Big Cypress voted. In 1959, 90 voted; in 1963, 93 voted; but in 1965, only 52 voted. The informant said:

> When we first started to vote, everyone voted, but little by little, people stopped. Last time there was a petition to put W.T. on the ballot, and twelve people signed, but only eight people voted for him. Everyone else voted for W.F., but a lot of people didn't vote at all. The nominees held parties to ask people to vote for them and to tell them what they would do for the people. People went to the parties but didn't vote.

This is not an attempt to compare the voting percentages from Big Cypress with voting figures from the general rural population, but rather a comparison of the voting percentage as it has decreased at Big Cypress from 1957 to the present.

Examining voting records of the election of May 10, 1965, and records of cattle ownership, I found that of the total of 28 eligible cattle-owning residents in that election, exactly half did not vote. The people not voting were the owners of the smallest herds with an average herd size of 49 head as compared to an overall average of 66 head. The voting owners, on the other hand, were those people who owned the largest herds at Big Cypress, averaging 87 head. No voting owner, it is interesting to note, had a herd *below* the minimum size of 50 head considered desirable by the agency experts. There was no other difference between voters and nonvoters in family type, sex, age, or education. Thus the economic factor is apparently the primary variable involved in political participation among the cattle owners. The elected leaders at that time were themselves in the voting segment, owning large herds, supported by people in the same economic category.

Since the number of people who vote seems to be declining, direct individual participation is declining. It is this trend which reinforces the development of a power elite. A factor which probably counteracts this trend is the general lack of self-confidence of the elected officials in taking any responsibility upon themselves for any major decision without first knowing it is approved by most or all of the people. It is this need on the part of officials to seek approval of the constituents that saves the individual voter from personal impotence. That, plus the fact that the officials do care about the welfare and happiness of others in the Big Cypress population.

Some people express feelings of a lack of control over the forces in their lives. Thus there are individuals who rarely or never vote. Their attitude is, "What's the use?" They have a high sense of alienation or anomie and a low sense of political efficacy. The most common form of protest is not voting, rather than voting against, for voting itself is alien to them.

Comments on voting are pertinent. One old man said:

> They [agency people] said we should vote. But I don't want someone to tell me what to do. Now we have that. I liked it better when we all talked first and there were no big shots.

A middle-aged woman:

> I will vote if someone comes who will put the tribe first and not be a dictator. It doesn't help to vote if there isn't anyone you want to vote for.

A young man:

> There isn't any particular person I trust. I would vote if I thought it would do any good, but it wouldn't.

An old woman:

> I don't tell anyone what to do, and I don't want anyone to tell me what to do. What good is it to boss people around all the time? If someone gets to be a leader, he forgets about the lower people. Who helps the lower people any more? I don't vote.

A middle-aged cattle owner (man):

> Sometimes I used to argue with the leaders, but they never listened to me. They want to change things too fast. I don't argue any more. It doesn't do any good. One person can't do anything. We should all agree. When we vote for a leader he thinks he can tell us all what to do.

The people who don't vote have greater feelings of helplessness and inadequacy than those who do vote. "Elected officials don't care about the people" is a common complaint. Also the nonvoters are apt to say, "I don't understand what is going on and no one explains to me." By contrast, the Indians who vote regularly show, by their comments, that they understand the purpose of voting in a representative form of political organization, and they express reactions which indicate that they feel their vote has some effect on the tribal government and decisions made on behalf of the community.

A middle-aged man whose name appeared regularly on the voting lists said:

> Yes, I vote. I voted for the present leaders. They do a good job, but we ought to be training some younger men for later. Our leaders do the things they have to do. It is not an easy job and lots of people complain, but no one has ever done a better job, and they can talk to the Indians and to the white men.

A young man:

> I voted in all the elections at Big Cypress. A good leader has to know different ways of doing things and he ought to be able to suggest things when we have problems. It takes education, and that is one reason I would vote for a woman, because we have more educated women than men.

A woman cattle owner:

> I have voted for the present leaders, and I like the work W.F. does as a leader. He always comes back and lets us know what they talked about. He does a lot of work.

A young male cattle owner:

> Our leaders have worked with the government and they can get along with almost anybody. They learn things and tell us about what they have learned. They have the idea of organizing the whole tribe so everyone works for the good of the people. But we need younger people with more education now. We need young people who can get along with the old people and not feel superior because of their education but use it understandingly.

Even the voting residents do not like to have a segment of the population left out, as the last quotation above shows. Everyone feels more comfortable about decisions if there is communitywide agreement. No one is so free from the tradition of unanimity to believe that the leaders ought to ignore the interests or wishes of any group. It troubles even the young men and women and the less-tradition-oriented Indians when there is essential disagreement with important decisions. The leaders themselves feel the weight of tradition in this respect. "We never vote when anyone is mad. We just talk and talk until everyone understands."

An officer of the Cattlemen's Association said:

I represent all the people who own cattle. Maybe people who are not interested and don't understand don't take care of their cattle, maybe they should not have bought cattle in the first place, but I am still their representative, and I am going to try to help them make a success. If a woman buys cattle, I feel the same way. I represent her and try to help her do the very best she can.

The Big Cypress member of the board talked about the problem of the disgruntled minority:

When we have a man who argues with us on something passed by the majority, I tell him that the board has voted, and since I was elected to be a director, I believe this is right, that what the majority wants is what everyone has to do. But if he still doesn't like it, I tell him to bring it up at the general meeting and maybe the majority will change the vote. But it is still hard when you know your people don't like something you have done.

Nevertheless, in spite of information meetings and frequent interpersonal contact between leaders and people, there are those Indians who never vote, never go to the meetings, and continue to complain that no one consults them and no one cares. Leaders have come to expect little opposition expressed through the medium of the ballot from these people, who on the other hand, will not support any decision or person either. Even the patient official will eventually reach the point of exasperation and tell a constituent that he, the official, knows best. The leaders will try to convince their constituents by quiet conversation and explanation, but time is more precious now than it was before the cattle program was initiated, and reaching unanimity may be impossible within the time limits allowed. The pressures of time and work acting upon the leaders may cause them to appear abrupt and unfeeling to some bewildered people. This response may heighten the belief that something is being "put over" on the people and that they are helpless to prevent it. The elected officials know very well who votes and who does not, and the leaders draw their support from the voting group. Unsuccessful candidates who have run in the past have not developed enough insight to recognize the existence of two clusters of residents, and often have overestimated the strength of their support because they have had verbal statements of agreement from people who never go to the polls. In consequence the losers have been chagrined to learn that they not only lost, but lost by a very wide margin.

# 7

# The Cattle Program
# and Acculturation

THE RANGE OF CHANGE in life-styles at Big Cypress shows clearly in the
adaptation to a major economic innovation, the introduction of stock
raising, and the implementation of the cattle program offers an opportunity to examine culture change in process. The amount of money involved,
the number of people affected, and the changes wrought by the program all make
it of crucial importance. Most families at Big Cypress have at one time or another
participated in the cattle program. An important aspect is that the program
created opportunities for income without challenging the Indians' noncommercial,
nonindustrial orientation, and cattle raisers were able to stay on the reservation
in familiar surroundings, an opportunity which residents valued. The cattle program has been their only opportunity to make an adequate living on home ground.

Experience and training in business and finance have benefitted a number
of people other than the cattle owners. The successes and failures of the program
have had major repercussions on the general standard of living and on cash
incomes. Even men who profess no interest in stock raising have followed the
development closely and have come to understand some of the problems of
financing a business venture on a large scale. Land use necessarily concerns all
the residents since land is tribally owned, and returns from land rentals should
benefit all inhabitants, not just stockmen. Jobs created by the extensive land
development are sources of revenue for some Indians, and as the land is built up
into improved pastures, community pride increases. Therefore decisions made in
the cattle program introduced more change into more aspects of Indian life than
decisions in any other sector of the culture.

## History of the Cattle Program

The Seminole Indians obtained cattle from the Spanish prior to the nineteenth century. However, during the Seminole Wars the Indians were constantly

on the move and could not care for the animals properly. In addition, as the people moved to the south, the environment changed, and ample pasturage was difficult to find. In the swamp areas where the Seminole sought refuge from the soldiery, oxen were occasionally used as draft animals, but other cattle could not live under the high water conditions.

By the early years of the twentieth century, white ranchers had begun raising cattle almost as far south as Big Cypress Swamp. The ranchers were versed in problems of water control, irrigation, and drainage. The Seminole learned some techniques by observing the ranchers, and suggestions were made to the federal government as early as 1917 that cattle raising might be an economic possibility. However, hogs were the only livestock raised in any number by the Seminole until the mid-thirties when the United States government purchased cattle from the western states hard hit by the drought and shipped the cattle to south Florida as a part of a national program for Indian economic development. Five hundred head of pure bred Herefords were shipped to the Seminole Agency. The cattle arrived in very poor condition; some were dead. More died during the drive from the railroad depot to Brighton Reservation.

Such was the inauspicious beginning of the cattle program, which was ridiculed because even the white ranchers in the area were not raising Herefords at that time. Hereford cattle were susceptible to certain diseases in the hot, humid conditions of southern Florida.

Under a trust agreement approved in 1939, the Commissioner of Indian Affairs appointed three Indian trustees from Brighton Reservation since there were no cattle yet at Big Cypress. If the range conditions were bad at Brighton, they were even worse at Big Cypress, and in order to be selected as trustee, a man was required to own cattle under the trust agreement. The state extension agent took on the job of extension worker for Indian affairs. The same man held that position while this fieldwork was under way. Concerning the problems of the late thirties, he said:

> There were a few people who could work as cattle hands. My job was to locate cattle on ranges, get minerals and ample pasturage and train workers. I had to teach the practice of weaning yearlings, rotating pastures, increasing the calf crop by using good bulls. The native range and climatic conditions were very bad— no drainage, much high water, and drought in winter. Everything was very difficult.

The herd was a tribal herd with the trustees representing the Indian people. In the forties, the federal government advanced money to purchase more cattle from an Apache reservation. The loan was to be paid back in cattle, one hundred head per year.

In 1946, the first trustees from Big Cypress were appointed. Native Florida Spanish cattle, generally considered low-grade livestock, were the only types that could be used in the swamp area at that time. The first herd numbered about one hundred fifty, and they were bred with water-tolerant Brahman bulls to produce calves adjusted to the local conditions. The original repayment program (accepting payment in kind) was national in scope, but the swamp ecology and range conditions produced cattle poorly able to adjust to conditions of the other reservations, and the Seminole were therefore encouraged to pay back the loan in cash.

As time went on, better practices of cattle management were introduced, and little by little a herd of about three-quarters Brahman breed was produced. In 1954, the herd was dispersed to individual owners, and livestock cooperative associations were formed. An improved range program was started by leasing the lands to commercial farmers and having the fields turned back to the tribe, planted with good pasture grasses and properly ditched and drained.

Range improvement and higher quality calves have been the two continuing goals of the cattle program. However, even with the aid in building up superior pasturelands through the leasing program, the cost of improving land is extremely high. Before 1963 the Bureau of Indian Affairs had been spending from $60,000 to $70,000 annually for land improvement, but by 1965, according to the state extension agent, maintenance cost was running over $200,000 annually. (These figures include both reservations.) In order to pay the operating costs, the grazing fees paid by the owners had to be raised, and the charges were assessed on a per head per year basis on an escalating scale. This financing was the subject of much debate and criticism.

## Problems of Indian Ownership

The aim of the cattle program is the production of marketable cattle fully comparable to the best product the white cattle ranchers of the area can breed. The production of such beef is dependent upon the maximum use of technical information on breeding, feeding, and marketing developed by the agronomists at the University of Florida College of Agriculture. South Florida has ecological problems which are extreme although by no means impossible of solution as demonstrated on the experimental farms which the state extension service and College of Agriculture support in the area. These experiment stations are run by highly trained agronomists using the latest scientific information and equipment. The Indians are neither highly trained nor, in some cases, even highly motivated. There have been Indian owners who have no real interest in becoming cattlemen: women who inherited cattle, old and disabled men, and those of all ages and both sexes who originally took a fling at cattle raising because they mistakenly expected to become rich with very little expenditure of labor. The Indians with an interest and aptitude which might someday allow them to become competitive stockmen have often been hampered by owners of very small herds, uneconomic cattle raisers, and by people who could not do or would not do the necessary work. The people with uneconomic herd size, that is, below fifty head, weighed down the program with a parasitic dependence according to the agronomists.

> Minimum numbers must be established to prevent people who are neither economically or philosophically ready to enter the livestock industry from starting herds so small as to have little chance for development and needlessly crowding

pastures. The limitation of available pasture makes it imperative that maximum and minimum criteria be established and strictly observed (Cattle and Pasture Regulations Article IV, Section A).

Until these new regulations were issued, it often cost the program more to maintain the participation of owners with herds below minimum size than could possibly have been paid back given the calf crop. Those below-margin owners could not increase the calf crop on the income of their undersized herds unless they were allowed to keep the calves to increase the herd size. However, if they did not sell their calves, they had no cash income at all, and therefore could not pay off the loan they had taken out. This is the economic conflict underlying the decision to introduce cattle keeping as a tribewide innovation. For the success of the total program, marginal owners simply had to be forced out. Some owners did not want to keep the yearling calves in order to attain an economic herd size. They constantly complained that they wanted income from cattle, and from their limited experience with the money market, they did not visualize an increase in herd as an increase in financial holding. Unaccustomed to investment, they thought only of money in the pocket. Such indiscriminate sales of calves and breeding cows for the purpose of producing immediate cash hurt not only the individual but had repercussions on all the cattle owners.

> . . . because the cattle operators have not yet reached the stage where they can fully pay for the cost of the pasture that they use, . . . the Board should regulate sales so that intensive methods of cattle raising will bring the greatest returns to the owners. In the past, personal demands, economic pressures and indiscriminate sales of brood cows have seriously restricted herd growth and many operators have therefore never attained cattle numbers sufficient to provide economic support (*Ibid,* Article III, Section A).

In order fully to pay the cost of pasture improvements and other advanced management practices, and to bring in an adequate annual income for a family, a total herd size should approach two hundred head per owner. This was considered an optimum unit in 1965 by the University of Florida and the state agricultural extension service. As already mentioned, the idea of delayed financial return is not always well received, or even understood. There are numerous complaints that the cattle bring no cash. Even though every owner has decreased the size of the debt still owed on his cattle, nine men said they had received no payment whatsoever during the years they owned cattle. "I have never gotten a cent, not even so small as a dime." The fact that he was paying off the debt from every sale meant nothing to this man. It is uncertain whether all owners really understood that they had a debt to pay off before they became clear and sole owners of the cattle. They just did not see decrease in debt or gain in equity as financial gain.

Another source of irritation was the pregnancy test. This procedure has been understood by only a few Indians. Many owners somehow became convinced that the pregnancy test was a sterility test, and if the cow had a calf another year, they felt that their belief that the test was inaccurate had been substantiated. A pregnancy test is merely an examination to see whether the cow is pregnant. If the cow is not, the agriculture experts want the Indians to sell the cow rather than keep her on pasture and pay a year's grazing fee for an animal that is not going to drop a calf. The experts say that it is better to sell, and then buy a replacement for the following season so that the grazing fee will not be charged. Carrying barren cattle over the year is a waste of pasture and work. On the other hand, proceeds from their sale can be used for replacement purchases later. Simple though the matter is, it has been unusually irksome to some owners. Even some of the more competent cattlemen consider the pregnancy test a nuisance and say that it should be abandoned.

The improved pastures have been accepted by most owners as better than native range, but not everyone has agreed. The development of improved pasturage has been a very expensive innovation and charges labelled "grazing fees" constitute the first deduction from income on sales. Frequently Indians see very little money, but very large charges on their sales. The one charge which appears to be excessive to them if not unnecessary, is the grazing fee. Therefore, they argue, why not use both improved pastures and native range. Use of both types of fields would reduce grazing fees, and they think that the quality of the product would not be lowered. It is a technical matter and one requiring education. The agronomists say that use of native range, even for part-time grazing, would cause the beef quality to deteriorate. The lines of communication between the technical specialists and the average owner are weak where scientific practices are concerned. It is very difficult to translate some scientific information which needs a lot of explanation in addition to translation. As one Indian who speaks English rather well put it:

> We should have this sort of thing explained to us. This is an example of what is wrong. We are not told enough about things. I don't think the white people at the agency can tell whether the translations are good nor not. Lots of times the government people talk a lot, but when the Indians translate it, they just say a little bit. I know they leave things out. Maybe they don't understand either and don't want to say so. I speak pretty good English, but I don't always understand the government people.

The experts explain to the officers and range riders, but the latter are hard put to explain to the cattle owners. At meetings, there are always official translators, but no agency employee knows enough Mikasuki to judge from his own experience whether the translations are adequate or not. The Indian leaders will usually take the word of the scientists on faith even when they do not understand completely.

> I do what Fred (the state extension agent) says to do. Even if I don't know for myself, he knows because it is his work.

The average owner does not have much contact with the agronomists because the agronomists contact the agency, not the Indians, and the Indian officials are not always able to convince other owners to do what the agronomists say. Unfortunately, the informational meetings are poorly attended, and the men who do attend are usually the owners who listen to the experts anyway. There is much misunderstanding at these meetings because of the problem in translating technical matters.

In addition to problems in technology there is general suspicion that the tribal officers are getting some sort of special treatment. This suspicion arises in part from the fact that the officers are in much closer contact with the white experts, and because the officers are also known to have the largest herds. Further irritation comes from a resolution passed August 18, 1958. It states that any cattle owner who is *also elected to tribal office* will not be charged a labor fee *if he is working on tribal business at that time.* For some undetermined reason, the ruling is badly misunderstood by almost every cattle owner, who usually takes it to mean that the board and council representative *never* have to pay a labor charge. The cause of the misunderstanding is hard to determine, but it is a sore that festers. Any mention of this ruling elicits responses which show how badly it is misunderstood:

> I don't know why the officers think they are special. They should pay like everybody else.

> It looks like the officers should pay since they are the ones who make the rules. I don't think it is right that some people pay and some don't.

> Officers should pay the same charges as the rest of us. They think they are big shots and don't work when the rest of the guys work. But what can we do? They make the rules.

More than anything else in the social philosophy, the Indians cherish the idea that they are all equal. The ten dollar a day labor charge for those who cannot or will not help at roundup is itself not approved by many Indians, but the idea that some have to pay it when they cannot leave their regular employment while the leaders are sometimes allowed to stay away without paying it, infuriates many of the other owners. This reaction is bitter, but the owners indicate that they have not sought an explanation from the Indian leaders. Although this resolution was passed by the leaders in their own favor without recourse to their constituents and indicates a move away from egalitarianism, it is also only a very small move in that direction. It was, in fact, a resolution encouraged by the superintendent at that time in order to make the position of leader more attractive because leader recruitment is not an easy matter. Many seemingly qualified Indians have stated categorically that they would never run for elective office.

Cattle owners, all of whom have work schedules for attending their cattle in the fields and/or corrals at roundup time, are often reluctant to take the responsibility for their own herds. Because of the expense, hired labor is avoided if possible, and each owner is expected to be responsible for work on his own herd. Some elderly, crippled or female owners must hire their labor. Even though they may be excused from roundup, the officers are far more apt to be at work on their cattle when their time comes for field work than many other owners. Some Indians acknowledge this fact.

> They've been working all the time, not only on roundup, but all year and going to meetings. The owners—a great many of them—don't come to round-up, so they have to charge, but the officers almost always come.

Not only do the officers observe the labor standards of white ranchers around the area, but they conform more nearly to the best husbandry practices in the general non-Indian population. The officers are concerned with both their own herds and the well-being of the total program. It is acceptance of major responsibilities of this sort that singled these men out as possible leaders early in the development of the cattle program. Their attitude is not to avoid as much work as possible, but rather to keep the program progressing at a good pace. When an owner fails to appear for roundup, the leaders must hire labor on his behalf, and substitute labor is not always easy to find at short notice. Then the owner will usually complain bitterly about being charged the labor fees for those times he does not appear. The inconsistency of refusing to care for their own herds, but expecting someone else to do it gratuitously is ignored by the owners. Records of attendance are kept by personnel from headquarters, so it is known whether men come at the appointed time or not. Cattle and Pasture Regulations, Article VI, Section A states clearly,

> The Board of Directors believes that cattle operators should assume full responsibility for cattle management and control. The Board and the Bureau will provide technical assistance and advice, and, in special or unusual situations, some direct service; but usually cattle operators will be expected to provide their own labor and adhere to sound pasture practices.

It is rare that the officers miss a roundup, for even when they have none of their own cattle involved, they go to roundups to supervise and to help the cattle manager.

## A Case History

As the following narrative shows, not all cattle owners are pleased with the program. Little Joe is an old man of about seventy years. He lives in a camp with another old man, his maternal parallel cousin. Neither man has a wife or children. In the summer of 1964 they had to leave their camp site because the Army Corps of Engineers had to build a major new canal there. After Little Joe and his cousin were paid a small sum for their chickees and small wooden shack, they built a new camp closer to the center of the village. With the money compensation Little Joe bought an old car. Since the new camp site had no safe water supply, he took out a water loan through the agency to pay for having a well drilled. He could, of course, have used the compensation he received on his campsite, but he had always wanted a car. Owning some cattle, Little Joe took out the loan for the well by himself instead of jointly with his cousin because cattle are necessary as security for loans. The new camp, like so many of the old people's camps, is attractively placed within a large clearing. The old people generally clear off a larger area and keep their camps more attractive than the young adults who are too occupied with their many children to spend time at beautifying a camp.

Little Joe got a loan for his first cattle in 1961. The cattle were his only source of income, for he was slightly crippled and too old to work in the fields. His cousin is an herbalist who gets some payment for his services. The payment is rarely in the form of cash, however. In 1965, Little Joe estimated that he owned 30 head of cattle, and the credit records at the agency showed that he actually did own 29 mature cows. Neither figure includes calves born that year, for they are not counted until September and market time. Little Joe kept a better accounting of his cattle than many old people, some of whom cannot count over 10. He had thought about owning cattle for a long time before he took out the loan.

> I decided that I would be able to pay off the loan by selling all the little calves and have money left over to spend for things. . . .

In answer to a question about whether he wanted a larger herd, he replied;

> No, I don't want any more. I am not paying off the loan fast enough, and I am not getting any money back like they said I would because it always goes into expenses, and I'm behind in my loan payments, and I am not at all satisfied with the program. I don't understand why they said it would be so different from what it is, and I can't find anyone who will explain it to me.

The Indians often refer to a mysterious "they," so the next question was to identify "them."

> Sometimes the people at Dania [now Hollywood], and our representatives said this too. But I don't like to ask about it. They might get mad. I don't want to bother people. They get mad at people who don't do what they tell them to do.

Although Little Joe said that leaders and people at the agency got mad, observation in the field did not show this reaction, at least as "mad" is commonly meant in American terminology. From answers to questions about the meaning of this term, it may be inferred that when a Mikasuki says mad, he means rather displeased. It is a very quiet, low-pressure response, but apparently very effective in its results. No violent or even forceful arguments or persuasive practices were observed during the fieldwork, but the thought of displeasing other individuals seemed to be an effective deterrent to questioning the leaders or other people about anything.

During the second interview, Little Joe brought out a sheet of paper and asked the interviewer to explain to him what was written on it.

> I have wanted to ask about this for a long time. I can't read, but I know I never get any money. Why is that? I don't understand how they make charges. My charges are always the same as the sale price, no matter what the sale price is. How can that be?

His charge sheet showed the following information:

| 1 cow | value | $92.49 |
|---|---|---|
|  | total gross sale | $92.49 |
|  |  |  |
|  | deductions |  |
|  | Grazing fee | –0– |
|  | Operating cost | 18.50 |
|  | Interest on Loan | 9.29 |
|  | Principal on Loan | 61.53 |
|  | Livestock commission | 3.17 |
|  |  |  |
|  | Total | 92.49 |
|  | Net to owner | –0– |

At the time he received this charge sheet he was not paying for his loan on the well or that would have been included under the heading "short-term loan." Livestock commission is paid by every cattle seller in Florida. It is a standard fee for marketing costs. After a visit to agency headquarters, I discovered the following list of charges on all cattle sales:

25% grazing fees
20% operating costs
40% loan payment
15% to owner

However, included in the *owner's share* of the 15 percent there are still other possible charges: 1. labor charges due; 2. house loans; 3. water loans; 4. short-term loans; 5. arts and crafts charges; 6. others. It took a literate anthropologist a day to get this information. It was almost impossible for an illiterate Indian (who did not even know where to go for information) to get an explanation. Because Little Joe was behind in his loan payment (due to a very small calf crop) all of his sales after operating costs and livestock commission had to be credited to repayment of interest and principal. This complicated accounting was very difficult for the old Indian to understand even when someone was willing to explain it to him. Even after explanation it is doubtful whether he really grasped the reasons for his lack of cash income. The interviewer saw many cash sheets with the statement, "Net to Owner —0—." Most of the recipients were as mystified as Little Joe. Some of the Indians, particularly old people who often cannot count beyond a dozen, asked the interviewer to go to the agency and look up the size of loan still to be paid off, and sometimes even the size of the herd owned. They not only cannot keep track of their own herd size and calf crop, but have no grasp of the magnitude of the debt owed. They do not understand percentages and, to go one step further, it may be assumed that they cannot conceive of the immense financial operation required to run a cattle industry. They understand only that their charges are so high that they absorb all the income from sales; therefore, the promises of "money left over to spend for things" have not been fulfilled.

Little Joe's case is typical of at least five other old people, and supports the contention that the agency personnel exert control over the Indians through the agency control of loans and repayment. This history also demonstrates the general unwillingness on the part of many Indians to ask questions about those matters which they do not understand. In those days, before the toll road, the agency was 120 miles away—quite a trip even for those motivated to seek an explanation. It is unlikely that the Indian representatives could explain the charges very well, for they are only semiliterate, and it is not the leaders who decide on the amount or distribution of the charges.

Not all cattle owners are puzzled by the charges. The range rider made the following statement about the costs:

The costs we have to pay are necessary to development. If the credit office decides that we have to pay more for some things after our sales, they know best. They have to help us with things like that.

But far more common are reactions like these:

I have never had any money after the loan and other charges are paid off. I heard that the owner is supposed to get 20 percent of what he sells. Then the charges are supposed to come out. I have never received a cent. I think I know what percent means, but a lot of Indians don't know what it means.

Grazing fees, livestock commissions and things like that take all the money. At the beginning I understood that I was to pay it back $600.00 every year, but it doesn't work that way. I just don't know what is going on.

I heard that we were supposed to get 20 percent of the sale before paying the bills, but we never get anything. I once asked in a meeting why I didn't get my money, but I was told that someone had put a stop to it, and it wasn't recorded in the minutes.

Sometimes the income is low. It's hard to say why. Everyone expected a lot more money than anyone ever got. I guess we didn't always understand.

I'm selling out. I am not getting nearly as much money as I expected, and I work very hard.

Article II, Section A of the Cattle and Pasture Regulations says:

These regulations or their amendment shall be subject to the approval of the Superintendent of the Seminole Agency.

The agency feels that control must remain in their hands until there are more educated and experienced Indian cattlemen.

## The Cattlemen's Association

Between 1959 and 1966, the Cattlemen's Association was an organization of all cattle owners on the reservation; membership was mandatory. There was a membership fee of five dollars, but no yearly dues. The association was organized to manage the cattle program in the field, as opposed to the financial management which is under the control of the Seminole Tribe, Inc., and the agency superintendent. There was a board of directors of five members elected by the membership on secret ballot. The directors met at least every 60 days, and there was an annual meeting for all members. The general membership was allowed to attend the directors' meetings, but there rarely were any members other than officers present except for the range riders who are employees in the pastures. The directors received no set salary but were paid ten dollars per meeting and given a gas allowance for travel.

With the guidance of the cattle manager (the state extension agent) the association had the responsibility for proper field management of the herd, rotation of fields, fence maintenance, bull service, etc., and was important as well in the education of the members in matters of scientific improvements. Special meetings were called to explain and illustrate breeding practices, medical care of cattle, mineral supplements, and the desirability of various breeds of cattle under southern Florida conditions. The educational meetings were conducted in English and translated into Mikasuki. It is quite likely that some of the information was not understood in translation, for many important points in scientific cattle raising appeared to confuse some of the people in spite of the discussions. Nevertheless, it was through the meetings that the average owner supposedly learned how to run and improve his cattle business. The president of the association attended information meetings at the state university in Gainesville to bring back data on livestock to the rest of the membership, but once again there were some translation problems, although, as will be pointed out later, technological changes were accepted more readily than financial changes.

The purpose of the association was to develop better beef through a combination of persuasion and example. The association had no real authority to enforce good management practices. In the case of pregnancy testing, for example, there was no enforcement of the test, and there was no way of forcing the owners to take care of cattle during roundups. The association did have authority to force common marketing because there was a signed agreement between owner and association, a contract to sell cattle cooperatively and to use only association owned bulls for breeding to maintain and improve the quality of the herd. The association assumed ownership of mavericks on the range, but otherwise it was primarily a marketing, educational, and advisory organization without powers of coercion. The owners have been under no legal obligation to care for their cattle or for the pastures which are tribally owned and are administered by the Seminole Tribe of Florida, Inc., through its land development enterprise.

The inabiilty to enforce good practices was a major drawback. After a great deal of discussion and difficulty, it was finally decided that the Seminole Tribe of Florida, Incorporated, would take over the direction of the cattle program for a four year period starting January 1, 1966. This decision was one result of the passage of new cattle regulations which put powers of enforcement in the hand of the tribal board. The cattle association, as mentioned, was merely an advisory, educational, and marketing organization. The board of directors of the Seminole Tribe, Incorporated, with the agency superintendent, became the decision-making organization. Under the new regulations, the state extension agent has the position of cattle manager under the general supervision of the agency superintendent but with wide latitude for independent action. The responsibilities of the cattle manager are spelled out in the Cattle and Pasture Regulations. At the time the new regulations went into effect, the actual leadership personnel was not changed, even though enforcement of the regulations was allotted to another organization, because the president of the board of directors of the cattle association was the Big Cypress representative of the tribal council, and the Big Cypress member of the corporation board was the vice-president of the cattle association. In effect, duplicated functions were eliminated and the responsibility for the success or failure of the program was concentrated in one group instead of being divided between two organizations. In giving overt prominence to the agency superintendent, the board of directors merely recognized a position of authority which had long been powerful but which had not always been publicly recognized as such.

Under the new regulations the tribal board has enforcement powers which it can bring to bear on recalcitrant owners. Beginning January 1, 1966, owners were required each year to sign a cattle raiser's agreement which clearly delineates rights, privileges, and responsibilities. The expectation was that a written agreement would stop the dissension and controversy arising from misunderstanding of the role of cattle raiser. Another written agreement must be signed by all owners in order to allocate the work involved in the pastures. A new work agreement will be made yearly as herd ownership changes. Penalties were levied starting in 1966.

A truly anomalous position is that in which the noncattle owners find themselves. They are not incompetent people. Indeed, it may be said that they have unusual strength of purpose to withstand the pressures on them to purchase cattle. However, they have held out against the main current of economic drift, and they are without organization or specialized leadership, whereas the cattle owners are members of a special interest group even if they participate in its activities little or not at all. There is no leadership for the nonowners outside of the representatives to the board and council of the tribe who are cattle owners themselves and whose primary interest, we may assume, lies in the success of the cattle program. The people who do not own cattle are in veritable competition with the cattle owners for the services and loans from the agency, but they usually find it hard to get attention without cattle, for the foremost demands made on the time and attention of the agency and the leaders stem from the cattle industry.

> It would be good to have something instead of just cattle, but I don't know what to say. People in towns have lots of different jobs, but what can we do down here? I never wanted to take care of cows, and that is all that the leaders are interested in.
>
> I would like to have a house, and there should be some other way of getting a loan than owning cattle. Why make me into a cowboy when I don't want to do that kind of work? I want to be a mechanic and learn all about cars. I am interested in that, and I would work hard at that, but not with cows.

Decisions made in developing the cattle economy may be classified into two basic types: those which involve changes in technology and those which involve financing. Technological development concerns changes in scientific management or equipment. Decisions on financial matters involve labor charges, grazing fees, and loan repayments. Decisions concerning financing may, of course, be made as a result of decisions to change technology.

Changes in technology have been made more easily and swiftly and have resulted in less discontent than decisions about financing. Changes in technology are more readily seen as beneficial, and the means to a desirable end is clearer. Answers to a questionnaire designed to test understanding of technological change indicated that most cattle owners did comprehend the reasons for changes in breed of cattle, introduction of pasture improvement, and so on. In answer to the question of why Angus bulls are used now instead of Brahman, the following responses are typical:

> Brahman do not have enough beef and are too rough. Angus have more beef and can be handled much easier.

> Angus are much better because they have more beef and they sell for more per pound. Brahman are wild and hard to control.

> Brahman are too thin. Angus are fatter. We cross-breed our cattle with Angus bulls to even things up.

In response to whether improved pasture is better than native range, the following answers are typical:

> The cattle are better off on improved pasture. On the native range the cattle get wild, and it is easier to find and see your cattle in improved fields. On native range the cattle get into hummocks and swamps and they have to be chased out.

> Improved pastures are better than native range. It is not so much work at the roundup and the cattle get fatter.

Out of 33 people answering these two questions, 27 knew why the change to Angus bulls had been made and agreed that it was a good change; 2 understood the reasons for the change, but thought Brahman were better nevertheless; and 4 did not know why the change had been made. Twenty-two owners thought that improved pasture was better and gave scientific reasons for their choice; 6 people, indicating by their answers that they did not understand the problem, thought native range was better and 5 owners thought that in view of the pasture shortage both types should be used rather than limit the number of cattle. However, these latter knew why improved pasture was superior.

Inconsistencies arise when finances enter the picture. Although 22 people could explain why improved pasture is better, of this group, exactly half said that improved pastures cost too much. Out of the group of 22, only 6 made statements that indicated understanding of the reasons for high costs in improving the swampland.

> All the improvements have produced better calves and it is worth the cost.

> It costs a lot of money to build good pastures down here.

> We have to spend a lot of money in order to feed the cattle a good diet.

Seeing no inconsistency between their two answers, people who thought improved pastures were better still answered about costs:

> The pastures cost too much. $18.00 per cow is too much.

> We should cut the costs of improved pastures. This is where we can save money.

Seven people, including the two leaders, could explain why the cash income from cattle sales was low, and they understood that they were paying off debts which they owed on the original cattle loan. All of the others said that they were very unhappy with the income (or rather lack of it), and some typical statements to this effect have already been quoted. Financial problems are more severe and puzzling to the Indians than technical problems.

Most Indians appear indifferent about financial contributions by the government in the form of aid, advice, and goods. This is not necessarily because they believe that the government owes it to them, rather their lack of concern springs from a lack of understanding. Several hundred thousands of dollars in aid means nothing because several hundred thousand means nothing to people who cannot grasp this order of magnitude. Younger people may actually be concerned with the size of the tribal debt (although not many evinced much concern), but many owners are much more interested in the fact that grazing fees might be raised by the sum of two dollars per head because they have to pay the two dollars, and it is a sum they understand. The apparent lack of gratitude toward the government is the result of inexperience in long-range planning and unfamiliarity with large sums of money. Many Indians have no idea how much the government has done at Big Cypress.

Decisions to introduce technological innovations have been supported by the extension agent at community meetings. Cattle owners trust the extension agent and believe that he knows best. Twelve cattle owners indicated that they would go to the extension agent for help and advice on cattle. Not one owner said he would go to agency personnel at Hollywood. The rest of the owners indicated that they would go either to the Indian leaders or to the Indian range rider, and the leaders and range rider were members of the group who said they would contact the extension agent. The extension agent is obviously an important figure to the Indians. Support for changes in financing comes from Bureau of Indian Affairs personnel who are less well known to the Indians. These men are also to some degree mistrusted by the Indians. The important point here is that almost all Indians consider these individuals as "authority" rather than as "experts." Advice from agency people is thought to have ulterior purposes. Indians say that these outsiders, unlike the extension agent, really do not understand their problems. This suspicion of agency personnel and Bureau of Indian Affairs representatives, coupled with the intricate and unfamiliar financial problems, has resulted in long delays over financial matters. Decisions in such a situation tend to be slow in the making, and the average owner has responded by resisting the implementation of these decisions. The Indian leaders know that decisions which do not have community acceptance will not be implemented by the cattle owners, and therefore the leaders procrastinate until they have persuaded the owners that the decision is beneficial. It is very important to point out that a swift decision on matters deemed important may be enough to arouse the antagonism of the people even if it is a decision which they might otherwise approve. The people like to be consulted, and important decisions made without consultation may cause the owners to react unfavorably.

Partial accommodations may be made to alleviate temporarily certain problems or conflicts. Examples of these stopgap measures are the use of some low-grade cattle rather than immediate total change to Angus, some pasturing on native range, and the leaders not forcing issues even when they have authority to do so. An officer of the Cattlemen's Association told me:

> We have the power to ask men to leave the association if they do not cooperate. But we have never used this power. This power would force a man to sell. If they decide to sell, that's up to them. The leaders do not try to force them out.

Another officer in the association said,

> It is best not to push too hard. Let people have time to think it over and get used to it. We let them go on doing things the old way for a while because everyone is happier if they have time to think it over. There are people in the cattle business who shouldn't be. Sometimes we have announced at cattle meetings that people are free to quit so that they will know we won't be mad. If they really don't care they should quit.

## The Decision on the New Cattle and Pasture Regulations

Major financial decisions are aimed at making the cattle program self-supporting. The decision to be discussed is probably the most crucial decision concerning the cattle program to date, involving not only the greatest controversy the program had ever produced, but also a complete revision and tightening up on the regulations of ownership and management.

By 1963 most available government loan funds had been used up. If the owners could not pay more of the cost of the cattle program, the improved pastures could not be kept up and therefore Angus cattle could not be raised. Only Angus would be competitive in the general Florida market. It was absolutely necessary to get more money or the cattle program would fail.

It was essential that changes be made to correct the financial situation, and many meetings were set up at which agency personnel and the extension agent explained the problem in detail and suggested possible solutions. All the solutions proposed would in one way or another reduce the cash income to individual owners. Men from the Washington office of the Bureau of Indian Affairs were sent out to participate in the discussions.

By the spring of 1965 nothing had been decided because of the adamant stand of the people in opposition to raising any of the charges. For two years the problem had dragged on, and it was primarily because it was a financial problem that no decisions had been taken. Pasture maintenance cost $218,000 per year. The Bureau had been contributing $100,000 per year, but that would not continue indefinitely. The tribe contributed $50,000 per year, and that still left $68,000 to be raised. The meetings intensified. A summary of the meetings between June 2, 1965, and October 6, 1965, when the board finally decided on a course of action, shows six general community meetings, eight cattle association meetings, six meetings of the tribal board of directors, and one special meeting with the State Director of Extension Services—a total of twenty-one meetings in five months, and these figures do not include the many informal and unofficial gatherings. The result was the new cattle agreement and pasture regulations, the full effect of which has yet to be assessed. However, by 1968, one result was a decrease in the number of cattle owners. Almost all the marginal owners were forced out. The new system required a change from a percentage of sales to a per capita basis for assessing grazing fees. To the experts, the new fee system was the only way out of the financial dilemma, but it took nearly three years to get enough support to pass the new program. Everyone agreed that it was the cattle owners' reaction to the grazing fee issue which created such a dilatory decision. In the end the owners did agree, but not until the grazing fees had been so arranged that they were put on an escalating scale on which the full amount would not be reached until 1969. The decision to approve these fees was not made until the situation had deteriorated almost to the point where it could not be remedied. This is a prime example of the lack of self-confidence on the part of the decision-makers. The decision could have been made three years earlier, but they feared the lack of community support. The need for wide consensus in Seminole society makes acting swiftly almost impossible.

It is instructive to look at a decision made concerning a technological change where no money was involved and the advantage of the change was quite obvious to all. At one meeting of the cattle association, the land operations officer from the agency showed by means of a number of pictures and charts how pasture rotation worked and why it was a good practice. His illustrations and reasons were accepted as logical, and the decision was made at the same meeting to pasture cattle according to the growth of the grasses and clover. Implementation of this decision was prompt and everyone has been generally satisfied. The need for pasture rotation as a means to better cattle nutrition was clear. On the other hand, the raising of the grazing fees as a means of financing land development was not clear. The average owner perceived the situation as one in which more money was being taken from his cattle income, and even without the new fees, the income from cattle was considered too low. As far as the Indian was concerned, paying off the original loan and paying for the land improvement of the reservation were not income. Income was clearly defined as money in the pocket of the individual, not a decreased loan principal.

This is not simply the consequence of lack of financial sophistication. Early in the cattle program, a decade or more ago, some rather unrealistic promises were made to Indians in order to get them interested in cattle production. People who are no longer at the agency apparently gave the impression that great wealth (great, at least, in Indian eyes) would be forthcoming from an investment in cattle without too much hard work on the part of the owner. The problems of cattle raising and its expenses were not revealed by the agency people. An informant put it this way:

> An agent from Washington encouraged me to get a cattle loan. As I understood it, I would make money and have an income. Maybe I could build a home. I would have security for the future. He didn't say how much it would cost.

The Indians think that many promises were made, but few were fulfilled. People inexperienced in modern marketing and financing could not be expected to anticipate all the problems involved in the change to a cattle economy. They feel they were deceived. The connection between the financial means and the productive end has been obscure to the Big Cypress people. Before decisions in matters as controversial as an increase in grazing fees are made, the decision-makers want to feel as secure as possible. That search for security may mean delaying decisions as long as possible until forces outside the Indian community become so great that the decision-makers can use these external pressures as an excuse for accepting the results of the decision.

Such a postponement may serve a psychological function. Decision-makers can point out to disgruntled constituents that they had no alternative and that they, the decision-makers, are as unhappy with the decision as the people themselves.

If this analysis is valid, then it is clear that if external pressures had not been brought by the non-Indian influentials, the decision to assess higher grazing fees would never have been made, and the Indian decision-makers probably could not have coped with the resulting financial problems. This at least is the opinion of the agency people, and it is the reason they give for their determination not to let the Indians take over the direction of the cattle program. The agency men fear that if they abdicated their guardianship, the cattle program would either collapse or would serve the selfish ends of a few, and the majority of the people would suffer.

The result is that the Indians are still financially dependent upon outside society in the form of the local agency and its fund-raising ability. This dependence carries with it a dislike and suspicion of the agency personnel and reinforces their belief that people at the agency in particular, and white society in general, are out to trick the Indians somehow. The agency dominance causes resentment on the part of the average cattle owner because he feels that his freedom of choice has been curtailed, as indeed it has. Consequently, although there is a great deal of admiration for the technology of the outside world, a genuine respect and liking for certain individuals, and a desire for more material goods, there is also a high degree of ambivalence toward white society in general. This is reinforced by the knowledge of the control which agency people can and do exert over the Indian and by belief that white men do not keep their promises.

The Indian officials are in a position between two groups, white society and reservation society. They cannot make decisions in the face of intense opposition on the part of their own people even though they know that the decisions must be made in order to implement the cattle program. However, the people do not react in the same way toward all segments of outside society. The extension agent for Indian affairs is accepted because he goes to the pastures and actually works with the Indians. The cattle owners are more apt to heed his advice than the advice from anyone else. On the other hand, the land operations branch of the agency which is in charge of the extension services has employees who do not see the Indians very often. Their only encounters are in formal situations such as meetings rather than out in the fields.

Indians know that there have been conflicts in the past between the extension agent and other agency personnel. The cattle owners think that the extension agent has a more realistic attitude toward their potentialities and that the agency people expect too much of them. When the experts do not agree among themselves, it is not surprising that the Indians are more confused than ever. It is also not surprising that the Indians are more apt to side with the man they know better and trust.

## Attitudes of the Owners toward the Cattle Program

The general attitudes can be assessed by considering two factors: (1) the number of people who have sold out, and (2) the number of people expressing great dissatisfaction.

All five men who had sold out by the time the new regulations had been passed gave as the major reason for selling the fact that the work was much too hard. One of these men was partially disabled, but the others were no less physically fit than cattlemen remaining in the program. Besides the discontent over the strenuous work, there was great dissatisfaction with the financial return. Comments among the sellers stating disappointment over income were common.

A few years back I got enough money to support myself, but lately there is nothing left after charges.

I've been at it for twelve years. I never paid off the first cattle mortgage, and I didn't have enough cows to make a living, and so I got a loan for more, but I wasn't making enough.

At the end the charges took all my money, and other people say this too.

Interviews with cattle owners remaining in the program pointed up similar dissatisfactions which, nevertheless, were not enough to make them sell out. However, after the passage of the new regulations, the minimum requirement of 50 head of cattle forced out all those who were unwilling to buy enough cows to bring their herd up to size. Expectably, there were many voices raised in anger about that requirement.

They said this was for everybody. Why did they make it so I had to sell out? I just didn't want to borrow any more money to buy more cattle.

Looks like some people are trying to get the little man out of the program.

I don't like it. There are some big shots around here. It's my business how big my herd is. The land is supposed to belong to all of us.

There have been numerous other complaints. Owners who have regular jobs off the reservation have found it impossible at times to attend roundups. They feel that it is unfair to be charged a labor fee when they cannot leave their jobs to attend to their cattle. Men with disabilities and women who cannot do physical work on the cattle have also objected to being charged a fee. However, there are arrangements for women owners to do substitute work like preparing meals for the cowboys during the roundups. Of course, to the more successful stockmen, it has been obvious that someone had to pay for the labor on cattle when the owners were unable to take care of them. However, to many owners, labor charges are unfair and they explain why their income has been disappointingly low.

No one interviewed was completely satisfied and enthusiastic about the cattle program. As stated, the two primary discontents were the low cash return and the hard work, but many other irritations were mentioned. Some people have not understood the need for certain technological changes; some people thought their calves were being stolen before they were properly branded; and there were a few people who seemed utterly opposed to any scientific change at all and thought it was better with unimproved pastures and scrub cattle because "even if they did not bring in so much at the market, those cows didn't cost so much and we never had to do any work with them either." Most owners are more realistic and consider the program partially successful. No one really claimed it was a total failure. If nothing else, everyone is proud because of the reputation they have gained from the experimental swamp drainage and change to pasture.

In addition to the many articulated dissatisfactions, there has often been unspoken discontent, perhaps best described as a general lack of feeling of accomplishment or participation, or helplessness and the inability to direct one's own destiny. However, in other cases, suggestions for improvements in the program have shown real awareness of the total problem. In addition to the officers and the range riders, the people who have had experience in catttle raising off the reservation have shown the greatest understanding of the situation. Those are the people who react to the problems in a constructive way. They are also the group that the agency people see as the future competitive stockmen, the group upon whom the success of the program depends. This group, with their spouses, also contains most of the voting population.

Although everyone expressed some disappointment, I was interested to note that very few of the informants indicated that they have in any way discussed the situation with other owners or have sought information or technical advice from experts. Those who have talked it over with each other or with the extension agent are once again members of that small group of owners who have at one time been in managerial positions or have had considerable experience working on white cattle ranches. The others, though often obviously dissatisfied, have made no attempt to discuss problems among themselves or with the officers. They have expressed themselves, if at all, by grumbling and innuendo, not by concerted action or discussion. If they do talk about their failures, it is to nonowners rather than to someone who might be able to help or explain.

Whenever the officers make decisions, the owners are informed by word of mouth or by writing, but even if the average owner is puzzled by or opposed to the decision, very few try to get an explanation for it. Less than a fourth of the total association membership indicated that they ever argue with officials or even discuss decisions at meetings. A few men, members of the experienced group, claimed that they tried to talk to officers privately but were not successful. The others felt that it was futile to talk to the decision-makers. "They never listen to us." "They just get mad when we ask questions, so I just keep quiet." These people considered the officers indifferent and unresponsive to the feelings and needs of the marginal owners. It appears that a sense of inadequacy and inferiority keeps owners from overtly attacking policy developed by the officials. The officers admit that the program is not perfect. But they are in command of facts unavailable to the average owner. They understand better the rationality of the program, the way the means are related to the ends, and they recognize that the cattle program is a long-range development. In other words, they are more realistic about the time, resources, and results. The officers and range riders can give an accurate account of the program for the next four or five years, an account that does not differ perceptibly from the expectations of the experts.

The attitude of the owners toward the Indian officials can best be described as one of ambivalence. A lot of vague discontent is directed toward the officers. The individual owner often does not understand enough of the total problem to be able to see the difficulties of decision-making. It is easier for the owners to blame the officers or the agency for their unhappiness than it is to comprehend the economic and managerial picture.

Although owners frequently indicate that a change in leadership would be desirable, very few are able to suggest alternative candidates. Almost everyone recognizes that certain qualities are essential, and tentative suggestions are frequently hedged about with such comments that "He doesn't speak English," or, "He would not work very well with the agency people," or "He is too old." There are not many people with leadership qualities. However, about half of the owners have indicated that they are reasonably pleased with their leadership, and the only reason they would like to see other people elected is to train more people to the task, although young men in a position of leadership are feared by many reservation people lest they become impatient and make rash decisions. Old age, too, has obvious restrictions.

During interviews, owners were asked how they felt about electing a woman official. Not even the women cattle owners thought that a woman could make a suitable officer of the Cattlemen's Association, but no one had any objections to having a woman as a representative from Big Cypress to the tribal governing bodies. When pressed to name names, no one could think of a woman at Big Cypress who would take the job, but two women were mentioned as candidates who would get some votes if they ran. When these women were interviewed, they were somewhat amused at the prospect of a career in politics, and they confirmed the belief that they would not run. However, the responses and attitudes seemed to indicate that there was no prejudice toward women in a decision-making position if they were otherwise qualified. The decisions made in the cattle industry were thought better left to men.

Attitudes of the people toward the decision-makers range from feelings of respect and admiration to jealousy and suspicion. Of all past officials one has always ranked high in the estimation of the residents. It is often said of him, "He helps the people." Another man, a former representative, is thought to have been more powerful in the sense that he was believed to have more "pull" with the agency. Selfishness or suspicion of selfishness is almost certain to turn the people against anyone. Some of the representatives have been "warmer" people, generally more warmly received by others. Sympathy and altruism will almost guarantee re-election, but an equally important factor in the maintenance of an elective position is the ability to communicate with the agency people on behalf of the rest of the Indians.

In general, the cattle owners focus their vague discontents upon the elected officials for situations beyond the responsibility or control of those men.

The officials offer a convenient target. They are there, and they are supposed to "do something." Whenever the people of Big Cypress need help with the world outside the reservation, they turn to a restricted number of men for assistance. It is an inescapable conclusion that when the representatives render this assistance, they are entrenching themselves. There are very few serious rivals to these men. Fewer than half a dozen men have been elected to office since reorganization in 1957. Two of these have held office for most of the time. Indeed, one of them has been returned to office every election. He has yet to be defeated. There is undoubtedly some jealousy in the universally acknowledged fact that the officers are more successful in their chosen career and in cattle raising than the average owner, and they also have better jobs, more material goods, and greater economic security. Some of the discontent can therefore be put down to envy.

## General Expectations

The cattle owner is not quite so naive as he was ten years ago, but there are still few men who have a truly realistic notion of what must be done in the future if the program is to become self-sufficient. The federal government still contributes almost half of the costs. The owners have been getting a much higher percent return on their investment than stock-raisers anywhere else in the United States, and that includes the great western ranchers too. They get this high return because the Bureau of Indian Affairs had helped to pay for the land development and because they get a very favorable loan rate. If the Bureau of Indian Affairs were to stop this subsidy, it is probable that the program would fail. Even the Indian decision-makers do not comprehend the problems they would face without government support. If the people feel that they have not been getting enough income from cattle, they have no conception of financial return under conditions of total independence. To this extent Indian expectations are still unrealistic.

The owners who have indicated willingness to put forth the labor and capital necessary, those who are really hoping to bring their herd size up to the economic unit of 200 head, no longer have any expectations of great wealth. They hope for financial security and a small estate to pass on to their children. Not everyone owning cattle can be classed with this group. Those owners who had fewer than 50 cows, either had to borrow to increase their herds to the minimum required by the new cattle regulations or were required to sell out. Most of the women and the elderly men were in this category. Those people were too naive in their expectations, although even they became more sophisticated as time went on. It seems probable that these people should never have been in the program at all, even if they had been willing to increase their herd size. Their incompetence put a drag on the program. The problem was that since they shared in the land as residents, they were entitled to the same rights in land usage as any other member of the tribe. However, the insistence on restricting the program to successful workers would have been more appealing had there been some other program by which those unsuited to the cattle business could make a living. People who are not in the cattle business have no other economic expectations. This has caused men and women to participate when they would have been attracted to almost any other form of livelihood. In addition, early in the program grandiose inducements were made to get everyone to participate. Everyone who believed the promises made at the time the cattle were released to individual ownership has been bitterly disappointed. There are no owners left who have such totally unrealistic visions, but it appears that even now there are some people who still do not understand all that scientific cattle raising involves if it is to be a success.

## 8

# Conclusion

## Summary

**T**HE FLORIDA SEMINOLE are descendants of fragmentary tribal groups dislocated by white soldiers and settlers who moved into the southeastern United States in the eighteenth and nineteenth centuries. Living in geographic and social isolation except for occasional trade contact with Anglo-America, the Mikasuki speakers, inhabitants of Big Cypress, maintained their language and many cutsoms intact until the decade of World War II. Following the end of the war, increasing contact with outer society, resulting from road and canal building in the swamp area, brought about many changes, slowly at first, but with increasing rapidity in the decade of the sixties.

Change involved the eager acceptance of many material items, and, more reluctantly, the introduction of new life-styles and economic patterns. The most sharply defined and far reaching of the changes occurred in the development of the cattle economy in the erstwhile swampland. The new technology went hand-in-glove with a new political organization, The Seminole Tribe of Florida, organized under the provisions of the Wheeler-Howard Act of 1934.

The Seminole Tribe of Florida, as a polity, is composed of Indians from three reservations: Brighton, Hollywood, and Big Cypress. Together they form one political structure which is based on ethnicity, not territorial contiguity. The members of the political unit speak two mutually unintelligible languages, but the tribal governing bodies (the council and the board) are the legislative, executive, and to some extent, the judicial organs for all three groups. Each reservation has its own representatives to the tribal council and board of directors. The feeling of "oneness" is derived from the common cultural heritage and to a lesser degree from their union against outside society.

There have been many difficulties and misunderstandings in the introduction of the ballot and majority rule. To many of the people, the vote is only remotely a means of choosing leaders or deciding issues. The people have not yet abandoned their tradition of decision-making through unanimity. The leaders do not initiate political action. Rather they consider themselves serving as the voice of the people. Since the agency is still an object of suspicion and is considered very unpredictable, the people prefer contact through the mediation of the elected officials, not because they were elected, but because the people believe that the officials will act on their behalf. The people may not be sure what the officials will say, but using them as negotiators is still preferable to talking for oneself. It is easier to have someone else take the responsibility, and the leaders are most efficacious in their position as arbitrator-negotiators. Their authority can be reduced to impotence within the community by the passive resistance of the residents. The legitimacy of the leaders' position is accepted by the people not because they were elected through the ballot, but because the leaders perform a valued service for their constituents. They act as spokesmen for the community and represent its interests before the rest of society. Herein lies the power of the decision-makers.

Individual autonomy in action, thought, and opinion is also a tradition. Joining committees and participating in civic organizations and service groups has never been a means to leadership or power among the Big Cypress people, and there are no organizations which could be considered means of recruitment for elites or as steps to power. However, while the leaders may not have any organized support, neither have they any fear of organized opposition. Big Cypress residents just do not organize into extrakinship and extrahousehold groupings.

Just as there have been difficulties in political change, so there have been problems in implementing the cattle program. The Indians' view of the situation was not correctly assessed by most agency officials. The individual Indian in the process of becoming a cattleman was almost from the beginning working under misunderstandings and misconceptions arising from lack of technological and financial training and lack of communication between the residents of the reservation and the agency personnel. The Indians expected a higher income than they had ever had, but they did not expect cattle raising to involve much work, and they certainly could not have foreseen the bewildering multiplication of costs—costs of grazing fees, bull service, veterinarian services, pregnancy testing, mineral dietary supplements, etc., which would be levied. They did not understand interest, principal, or percentage. Thus they often became disillusioned.

From the beginning the agency personnel and the Indian cattle owners (with the possible exception of the Indian leaders) had different views of what constituted proper economic gain. The agency saw it as maximizing the return, and the Indians saw it in terms of sufficing. The Indians never planned to squeeze as much out of the cattle industry as they possibly could. They preferred a happy medium between physical labor and financial return. They were willing to receive less of the latter because they did not want to expend as much physical effort as the agronomists thought they should. The Indians were sometimes charged with laziness. The Indians, seeking a pleasant life, did not aspire to the same income that many white people wanted and they did not want to spend their days in strenuous physical labor.

The men who are becoming competent stockraisers are learning work habits and scientific techniques, but even they have not learned to handle their financial situation. If the program is to be successful, marketing and account keeping should be done either by individuals for their own herds, jointly through the tribe, or by some sort of hired business manager. At present the office of credit at the agency handles all accounts and oversees the marketing. It may be that this degree of self-sufficiency is impossible of attainment until a generation of Indians has gone through enough schooling to have learned business management and accounting. The work in the fields does not require literacy, but the financial aspect of cattle raising does.

Unfortunately house mortgages are tied in with the ownership of cattle as collateral. If an Indian had enough money to buy a house outright, he would not need cattle as security. But no Indians have this kind of money at present. Therefore, the Indians are figuratively right when they say that they have to have cattle in order to get a house.

No one is receiving enough money from cattle to be free of the need of another source of income. However, there are some owners who have close to an optimum size herd. If these people are able to produce a calf crop of 80 percent, they will stand as proof that cattle raising can be a successful way to earn a living at Big Cypress. The people who dreamed of becoming rich on cattle now realize that it was just a dream. Those who could not stand the labor have been forced out. New cattle regulations were designed not to deprive any Indians of their just return from land use, but rather to safeguard the program for those who could make a success of it. Some of the small owners who were forced out were rather relieved to be freed of the responsibility. Others doubtless felt that they had been cheated or tricked somehow because the program was built up in such glowing terms in order to induce them to participate in the first place. The Indians did not expect to live just like the white ranchers, but they certainly did expect to raise their standard of living considerably. The people who are staying in the program still hope for this, but now they know that it will take a long time and a lot of hard work.

## Implications for the Future

Big Cypress is becoming less and less self-contained. It is increasingly dependent upon the economic forces at work in the larger society. As workers gain employment off the reservation and as access to the general society is facilitated geographically by the new road and socially by education, individual residents will depend less upon the leaders as mediators and will show more effective opposition and political competition. The negotiator-arbitrator model will no longer be an accurate description of the power structure. There will be less need for buffers between the outside and the people, and when the leaders are no longer useful as mediators, they will have lost an important, or perhaps their only real, source of power within the community. The way the leadership role of the future is played will have to change. It is predictable that the leaders of the future will be increasingly initiators of change, leaders in fact as well as in title. It appears highly likely that there will be campaigns in which better educated people run for office on platforms of directed change.

It also appears probable that unless some new sources of income on the reservation are found, the more aggressive and competitive of the younger generation will make their home elsewhere near higher paying jobs. The inevitable conclusion must be that there will be increasing social stratification as the successful cattlemen become the economically dominant group, and the gap between their incomes and those of the rest of the population widens. In addition, the stockraisers will be politically as well as economically dominant. At present although there is a positive correlation between income and leadership, they are not in a cause and effect relationship, but rather are both indicators of the willingness and ability to conform to economic patterns of the dominant society. However, the connection between success in stockraising and political activity has been demonstrated. It seems unlikely that this correlation will lessen in the future. The cattle owners who vote have been those with the largest herds and therefore the largest capital investment in the project. They are members of the highest income group at Big Cypress. The economic factor is clearly the most significant variable in modern political participation among the Mikasuki. Therefore we may expect the trend toward political centralization by economic class to be intensified under the new cattle and pasture regulations as economic differentiation increases. Already the new regulations have resulted in limiting the cattle program to people who could make a success of it. This alternative was considered preferable to continuing the struggle against the retarding effects of cattle owners who could not or would not carry their share of the financial and managerial burden. But the choice was complicated by the fact that the cattle program offers the only economic potential on the reservation. The consequences of not participating in the cattle program are either economic difficulties and low standards of living, or else exodus from the reservation. Either alternative will increase the already incipient stratification.

# Recommended Readings

BARTRAM, WILLIAM, 1958, *The Travels of William Bartram*, Naturalist's Edition. New Haven, Conn.: Yale University Press.
Bartram was a botanist and ornithologist who traveled through the southeast in the 1770s while Florida was a British possession. The book contains many descriptions and comments about Indian life of the time.

GARBARINO, MERWYN S., 1970, Seminole Girl. *Trans-action*, 7 (4): 465–470.
An account of a Seminole woman who returned to the Big Cypress reservation after having achieved a business college education.

MACCAULEY, CLAY, 1884, *The Seminole Indians of Florida*. Annual Report, Bureau of American Ethnology, No. 5. Washington, D.C.: Smithsonian Institution.
The first ethnographic account of the Florida Seminole.

MCREYNOLDS, E. C., 1957, *The Seminoles*. Norman: University of Oklahoma Press.
A history of the removal of the Seminole from the Southeast to Oklahoma. The emphasis is on the Oklahoma groups although there is information on the early history of the Florida people.

STURTEVANT, WILLIAM, 1960, "A Seminole Medicine Maker." In Joseph B. Casagrande, ed., *In the Company of Man*. New York: Harper and Row. A biographical sketch of a Big Cypress resident and "medicine man."

SWANTON, JOHN, 1946, *The Indians of the Southeastern United States*. Bulletin, Bureau of American Ethnology, 137. Washington, D.C.: Smithsonian Institution.
A general description and brief history of southeastern tribes and their changes in historic and prehistoric times. Included is information on language, material culture, subsistence, religion, and social organization.

# References

BARTRAM, WILLIAM, 1958, *The Travels of William Bartram*, Naturalist's Edition. New Haven, Conn.: Yale University Press.

COLLIER, JOHN, 1947, *Indians of the Americas.* New York: Mentor.

DRIVER, HAROLD, 1961, *Indians of North America.* Chicago: University of Chicago Press.

GARBARINO, MERWYN S., 1967, "Decision-Making Process and the Study of Culture Change." *Ethnology.* 6 (4): 465–470.

———, 1970. Seminole Girl, *Trans-action.* 7 (4): 40–46.

MacCAULEY, CLAY, 1884, *The Seminole Indians of Florida.* Annual Report, Bureau of American Ethnology, No. 5. Washington, D.C.: Smithsonian Institution.

NASH, ROY, 1931, *Survey of the Seminole Indians of Florida.* 71st Congress, 3d Session, Senate Document 314. Washington, D.C.: Government Printing Office.

OBER, FREDERICK P., 1875, "Ten Days with the Seminoles." *Appletons' Journal* 14.

POTTER, WOODBURNE, 1836, *The War in Florida.* Baltimore: Lewis and Coleman.

SEMINOLE INDIAN AGENCY, Hollywood, Fla., 1913–1918, Annual Report to the Commissioner.

SEMINOLE TRIBE OF FLORIDA, Hollywood, Fla., 1957a Amended Constitution and By-Laws.

———, 1957b Amended Corporate Charter and By-Laws.

———, 1965, Cattle and Pasture Regulations.

SKINNER, A., 1913, "Notes on the Florida Seminole." *American Anthropologist* 15.

SPENCER, LUCIEN A., 1913, Special Report of Lucien A. Spencer, Special Commissioner to Negotiate with the Seminole Indians in Florida, April 1, 1913. Hollywood, Fla. Mimeograph.

STURTEVANT, WILLIAM, 1954, "Medical Practices of the Mikasuki Seminole." Unpublished Doctoral Dissertation, Yale University.

———, 1960, "A Seminole Medicine Maker." In Joseph B. Casagrande, ed., *In the Company of Man.* New York: Harper & Row.

SWANTON, JOHN, 1922, *Early History of the Creek Indians and Their Neighbors.* Bulletin, Bureau of American Ethnology, No. 73. Washington, D.C.: Smithsonian Institution.

———, 1925a *Social Organization and Social Usages of the Indians of the Creek Confederacy.* Annual Report, Bureau of American Ethnology, No. 42. Washington, D.C.: Smithsonian Institution.

———, 1925b, *Religious Beliefs and Medical Practices of the Creek Indians.* Annual Report, Bureau of American Ethnology, No. 42. Washington, D.C.: Smithsonian Institution.

———, 1946, *The Indians of the Southeastern United States.* Bulletin Bureau of American Ethnology, No. 137. Washington, D.C.: Smithsonian Institution.